MW00640095

The Readable Bible

Minor Prophets

From Iron Stream Media

The Readable Bible will be available as a complete Bible, in portions, in individual books as below, and as a twenty-seven volume set.

The Holy Bible	978-1-56309-531-3

The Readable Bible: Pentateuch

The Readable Bible: Genesis	978-1-56309-578-8
The Readable Bible: Exodus	978-1-56309-579-5
The Readable Bible: Leviticus	978-1-56309-580-1
The Readable Bible: Numbers	978-1-56309-581-8
The Readable Bible: Deuteronomy	978-1-56309-582-5

The Readable Bible: Historical Books

The Readable Bible: Joshua, Judges, Ruth	978-1-56309-583-2
The Readable Bible: 1 and 2 Samuel	978-1-56309-584-9
The Readable Bible: 1 and 2 Kings	978-1-56309-585-6
The Readable Bible: 1 and 2 Chronicles	978-1-56309-586-3
The Readable Bible: Ezra, Nehemiah, Esther	978-1-56309-587-0

The Readable Bible: Wisdom Books

The Readable Bible: Job	978-1-56309-588-7
The Readable Bible: Psalms	978-1-56309-564-1
The Readable Bible: Proverbs, Ecclesiastes, Song of Songs	978-1-56309-565-8

The Readable Bible: Prophets

The Readable Bible: Isaiah	978-1-56309-589-4
The Readable Bible: Jeremiah, Lamentations	978-1-56309-590-0
The Readable Bible: Ezekiel, Daniel	978-1-56309-592-4
The Readable Bible: Minor Prophets	978-1-56309-593-1

The Readable Bible: New Testament

The Readable Bible: Matthew	978-1-56309-566-5
The Readable Bible: Mark	978-1-56309-567-2
The Readable Bible: Luke	978-1-56309-568-9
The Readable Bible: John	978-1-56309-570-2
The Readable Bible: Acts	978-1-56309-571-9
The Readable Bible: Romans	978-1-56309-572-6
The Readable Bible: 1 and 2 Corinthians	978-1-56309-573-3
The Readable Bible: Galatians–Philemon	978-1-56309-575-7
The Readable Bible: Hebrews–Jude	978-1-56309-576-4
The Readable Bible: Revelation	978-1-56309-577-1

Visit www.ironstreammedia.com for more information.

The Readable Bible

Minor Prophets

Hosea, Joel, Amos, Obadiah, Jonah, Micah, Nahum, Habakkuk, Zephaniah, Haggai, Zechariah, Malachi

Translated and Edited by
Rodney S. Laughlin
Brendan I. Kennedy, PhD

IRON
STREAM

Birmingham, Alabama

The Readable Bible: The Minor Prophets

Iron Stream
An imprint of Iron Stream Media
100 Missionary Ridge
Birmingham, AL 35242
www.ironstreammedia.com

Copyright © 2022 by Rodney S. Laughlin

Library of Congress Control Number: 2022938636

Cover design: twoline || Studio

Interior designer/illustrator: Clyde Adams (www.clydeadams.com)

Map geographic features courtesy of Bible Mapper (www.biblemapper.com).

Typeface: Veritas AE from Altered Ego Fonts, a division of Aespire

1 2 3 4 5—26 25 24 23 22

Contents

Hosea

Joel

Amos

Part 1. Pronouncement of Judgment

Part 2. Prophecies Against Israel

Obadiah

Jonah

Micah

Part 1. The Lord's Judgment

Part 2. Direct Instructions and a Prediction

Part 3. Undated Prophecies

Malachi

Preface

To the Reader

One day I was standing in an airport bookstore looking for a book to read. I asked myself, "Why am I looking for something to read when I have a Bible in my briefcase?" I answered, "The Bible is hard to read. I want to read something easier." Then I asked myself, "Why is it so hard to read? You're a seminary graduate, a former pastor, a Bible teacher!" Thus began a quest that has led to The Readable Bible—the Bible as it would look if Moses, Joshua, Matthew, Mark, Paul, and the other writers had been sitting in front of a computer when God spoke through them.

It seems to me that the Bible is hard to read because all material is presented in sentence format. Today we use tables to present census information and charts for genealogies. When we want something built, we draw up a specification document. Law codes are organized in outline form. We use bullet points, bold text, and other aids to help us grasp information. Yet in today's Bibles, all the information is still presented in sentence format in plain text. Surely those men of old would have used modern formats if they had known about them when God spoke through them. Modern formatting does not change the information; it simply presents it in a way that makes it easier to grasp. The Readable Bible brings you the biblical text in modern formats.

You may struggle with the idea of Scripture in modern formats. Actually, all of today's Bibles present the text in a form much different from that of the original manuscripts. Consider how many format changes that were developed over the past two thousand years led to the format considered normal today. Each change was radical in its time:

- Vowels: The earliest Hebrew manuscripts have no vowels; they were added hundreds of years later.
- Capital Letters: The Hebrew Old Testament and the Greek New Testament manuscripts have no uppercase and lowercase letters.
- Punctuation: The original manuscripts have no punctuation (no commas or periods!).
- Chapter Numbers: These were not common in Bibles until the thirteenth century AD.
- Verse Numbers: The first verse-numbering system was developed over a thousand years after the last Bible book was written. It had one-third of today's verse numbers, making verses three or four times longer. Today's Christian Bible numbering system was not developed until the sixteenth century.
- Paragraphs: The first paragraphed King James Bible was published in the mid-1800s.

So presenting the words of Scripture in tables, cascading the text of long, complex sentences, and using other modern formatting techniques is simply continuing the long-term trend of making the Bible easier to understand.

Our hope is that people who have never read the Bible will decide to read this version because it is so approachable. Please give a copy to someone who struggles to understand the Bible and, especially, to those who do not read the Bible.

Acknowledgments

My thanks to all the members of our editing team, our volunteer development team, and the many others who have donated funds and worked to bring The Readable Bible to completion.

A big "thank you" to my designer and partner in this project, Clyde Adams, for joining me in this faith venture. He has turned the translation into well-laid-out text and my formatting concepts into reality. The maps, tables, charts, book layout, and cover are all his work.

Most of all, I thank my wife, Rebecca, for her ideas, her love, and her strong support of this endeavor over the past twelve years.

Dedication

And now I dedicate to our Lord this translation of his holy Word, humbly asking him to grant that it may bring forth fruit to his glory and the building up of his people.

Rodney A. Laughlin

Spring 2022

Introduction to the Old Testament Prophets

Old Testament prophets were spokespersons for God, proclaiming the will of God. Sometimes God gave them a vision or understanding of the future, and depending on what that future held, they warned or encouraged people by telling them what God had said.

Generally, the prophets' lives were lonely ones. They typically felt alone in their faith—sometimes they had to proclaim that judgment was coming, making them quite unpopular among a people who were enjoying their rebellion against God. Other times they had to proclaim that, though everyone had given up hope, God would restore Israel. Such preaching led to isolation, abuse, and ridicule by both kings and commoners.[a] Nevertheless, they stood for God regardless of the consequences.

The prophets were only people, just like us. They had moments of doubt, waning faith,[b] and self-pity.[c] They sometimes wanted to quit[d] and cried out to God for relief, even for vengeance on their enemies.[e]

God used the prophets for many purposes, to
>   correct people,
>   >   call them to repentance and a restored relationship with him,
>   encourage them,
>   reveal truths about himself and his creation,
>   tell people what he wanted them to do,
>   reveal actions that he was going to take (e.g., pronounce judgment or blessing),
>   announce who he had appointed as Israel's leader, and
>   lay a foundation of knowledge to help people recognize the coming
>   >   Messiah, Jesus.

God revealed coming events to some prophets. While informing the people about the future was important, it was a small part of the prophets' overall ministries. Every prophecy's foundational purpose was to bring people back to a walk with God by strengthening their faith. Predictive prophecy (and the recording of it) was to strengthen future generations in their faith, confirming that the past, present, and future are all within the knowledge and control of God.

The prophetic books record not only the words God spoke to and through the prophets but also the thoughts of the prophets themselves and the people to whom they spoke. When there is an unclear or abrupt change in the source of the words, The Readable Bible alerts you with an italicized lead-in (e.g., "*And I replied …*").

In the prophetic books, "Declares the Lord" occurs several hundred times within prophetic utterances. It is often unclear whether the expression is a comment of the prophet or words of God. It usually means "this is a solemn declaration/message." Except in cases where the expression is clearly words of the prophet, in prophetic books it is punctuated as words of God.

---

a   See 1 Kings 22:26–27.
b   See Exodus 4:1–13.
c   See Jeremiah 15:10.
d   See 1 Kings 19:1–4; Jonah 4:1.
e   See Jeremiah 11:19–12:4.

Introduction to the Minor Prophets

The Minor Prophets are so named simply because of the length of these books, not because of the writers' significance. The writings of these twelve prophets are short enough to be copied together on a single scroll comparable in length to one of the Major Prophets (i.e., Isaiah, Jeremiah, and Ezekiel). Profound theology,[a] beautiful poetry,[b] and striking, memorable images[c] are found within the Minor Prophets. Jesus and the New Testament writers quoted from them often.[d] Their importance to biblical revelation is certainly not minor.

The twelve minor prophets were active throughout several centuries in diverse places from Jerusalem to Babylon. As seen in the table below, God's message through each prophet was directly related to the spiritual condition of his target audience.

It is difficult to date when the prophets were ministering, so scholars differ in their dating. The ranges in the table below encompass the broader possibilities within which they ministered for some years. For more information, read Note on Dates of Events in the back matter of this book.

The Minor Prophets				
Date	Location	Prophet	Theme	Reason Message Needed
758–710 BC	Northern Kingdom of Israel	Hosea	Judgment against Israel's spiritual adultery	Israel was worshiping idols and plunging toward destruction by Assyria.
935–796 BC, or sometime in the 600s or 500s BC	Uncertain: most likely Judah	Joel	Meditation on repentance and restoration	A locust plague and famine were threatening those who returned from exile.
793–740 BC	Northern Kingdom of Israel	Amos	Denunciation of social and economic sins	Israel was corrupt and on the brink of annihilation by Assyria.
855–840 BC, or 627–586 BC	Edom, Judah's neighboring country to the southeast	Obadiah	Judgment for cruelty inflicted on survivors after fall of Jerusalem	Neighboring nations brutalized and enslaved Israelites.
800–750 BC, or about 400 BC	Nineveh, the capital of Assyria	Jonah	God's patience and desire for all to repent	To teach that God is active outside Israel and concerned for the Gentiles

a   See Micah 6:8.
b   See Zephaniah 3:14–17.
c   See Amos 5:24.
d   See Matthew 2:6,15; 9:13; 10:35; 11:10; 21:5; 27:10; Mark 14:27; Luke 11:29–30; 23:30; Acts 2:17–21; Hebrews 10:37–38; 12:26.

The Minor Prophets (*continued*)

Date	Location	Prophet	Theme	Reason Message Needed
750–686 BC	Southern Kingdom of Judah	Micah	Judgment of social and economic sins	Judah is corrupt and threatened by Assyria.
663–610 BC	Nineveh, the capital of Assyria	Nahum	Denunciation of cruelty and arrogance of a foreign nation	God is active outside Israel and will judge the Gentiles.
650–589 BC	Southern Kingdom of Judah	Habakkuk	Questioning God's justice	Judah is corrupt and God appears not to care.
640–609 BC	Southern Kingdom of Judah	Zephaniah	Judgment of idolatry and spiritual complacency	The people are corrupt even though the king is faithful.
520 BC	Jerusalem in the Persian province of Judah	Haggai	Encouragement to finish rebuilding the temple	The Jews have been intimidated into stopping work on the temple.
520 BC	Persian province of Judah	Zechariah	Predictions of restoration of Judah, the coming Messiah, and the day of judgment	Jews have begun to return to the land; hopes are high for a return to independence.
450–420 BC	Persian province of Judah	Malachi	Denunciation of social sins and failure to follow God's law	Descendants of those who returned from exile have become corrupt.

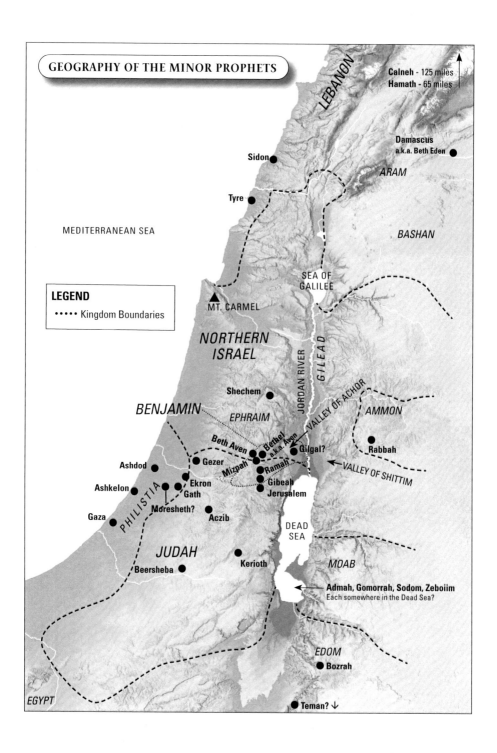

GEOGRAPHY OF THE MINOR PROPHETS

Calneh - 125 miles
Hamath - 65 miles

LEBANON

Damascus
a.k.a. Beth Eden

Sidon

ARAM

Tyre

MEDITERRANEAN SEA

BASHAN

SEA OF
GALILEE

LEGEND

•••• Kingdom Boundaries

MT. CARMEL

NORTHERN
ISRAEL

GILEAD

JORDAN RIVER

VALLEY OF ACHOR

BENJAMIN

Shechem

EPHRAIM

AMMON

Beth Aven

Bethel
a.k.a. Aven

Gilgal?

Rabbah

Ashdod

Gezer

Mizpah

Ramah

Ekron

VALLEY OF SHITTIM

Ashkelon

Gath

Gibeah

Jerusalem

Gaza

Moresheth?

Aczib

DEAD
SEA

JUDAH

Kerioth

MOAB

Beersheba

Admah, Gomorrah, Sodom, Zeboiim
Each somewhere in the Dead Sea?

EDOM
Bozrah

EGYPT

Teman? ↓

Before You Read

Words in *italics* are additions to the biblical text. In the context of commands, rules, and regulations, "shall," "must," and "are/is to" are equal terms, all the same strength.

Read lists from top to bottom in the first column then read the next column.

We encourage you to read "Translation Notes" and "Format and Presentation Notes" in the back of the book. They are easy reading and will increase your understanding of the text.

Please browse the glossary before you begin reading. You will find helpful information about words that appear frequently in this book, as well as important explanations of the words "Lord" and "Yahweh."

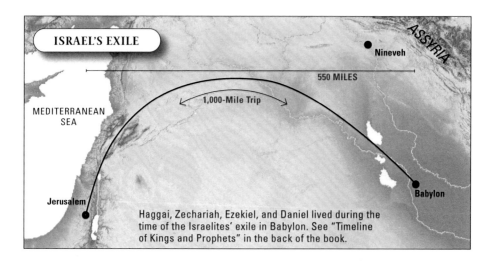

ISRAEL'S EXILE

ASSYRIA

Nineveh

550 MILES

1,000-Mile Trip

MEDITERRANEAN SEA

Babylon

Jerusalem

Haggai, Zechariah, Ezekiel, and Daniel lived during the time of the Israelites' exile in Babylon. See "Timeline of Kings and Prophets" in the back of the book.

Hosea

¹ The word of the Lord that came to Hosea son of Beeri in the days of[a] Uzziah, Jotham, Ahaz, and Hezekiah—kings of Judah—and in the days of Jeroboam son of Jehoash, king of *Northern* Israel.

Hosea's Wife and Children

² When the Lord first spoke through Hosea, the Lord said to him,
"Go, marry a whore and father children with her,[b] for the land has engaged in rank prostitution, turning away from the Lord." ³ So he married Gomer daughter of Diblaim, and she conceived and bore him a son. ⁴ The Lord told him, "Name him Jezreel (*i.e.,* God Sows), for in a little while I will punish the house of Jehu for the massacre *he committed* at Jezreel.[c] I'll put an end to the kingdom of the house of *Northern* Israel. ⁵ On that day I will break *Northern* Israel's bow in the Valley of Jezreel."

⁶ Gomer conceived again and had a daughter.[d] The Lord said to Hosea,
"Name her Lo-Ruhamah (*i.e.,* Not Loved), because I will no longer show compassion to the *Northern* Israelites, that I should forgive them at all. ⁷ But I'll have compassion on the house of Judah and deliver them—*I* the Lord their God—but not by bow or sword or in battle or by horses and horsemen."

⁸ After she weaned Lo-Ruhamah, Gomer conceived and gave birth to another son. ⁹ The Lord told her,
"Name him Lo-Ammi (*i.e.,* Not My People), because you are not my people and I am not your God. ¹⁰ Yet the number of the Israelites will be like the sand of the sea, which cannot be measured or counted. In the place where it was said to them, 'You are not my people,' it'll be said to them, 'You are children of the living God.' ¹¹ The people of Judah and the people of *Northern* Israel will be gathered together and have one leader over them.[e] They'll come up from the land, for the day of Jezreel will be great.

Israel's Unfaithfulness Condemned

¹ "Refer to your brothers as 'Ammi' (*i.e.,* My people), and to your sisters as 'Ruhamah' (*i.e.,* Beloved).

² "Contend with your mother *Israel*; contend *with her,*
     for she is not my wife, and
     I am not her husband.

---

a   Literally, "the days of."
b   Literally, "Go, take for yourself a wife of prostitution, and beget children of prostitution."
c   See 2 Kings 10:6–11.
d   The Hebrew makes it clear that this child and the child in verse 8 were not Hosea's.
e   Literally, "they'll appoint one head for themselves."

Let her remove
    the *look of* prostitution from her face and
    the adultery from between her breasts,
³ or I will
    strip her naked and expose her like the day she was born,
    make her like a desert,
    put her in a waterless land, and
    slay her with thirst. ⁴ I will
    have no compassion for her children,
        for they are children *conceived* of prostitution.
            ⁵ For
                their mother engaged in prostitution, and
                she who conceived them has acted shamefully.
                    She said, 'I'll go after my lovers who give me my food and water,
                    wool and linen, oil and drink.' ⁶ Therefore, look,
I will
    block her way with thorns and
    build a stone wall against her, so she cannot find her paths.
⁷ She will
    chase her lovers but not catch up to them,
    seek them but not find them. Then she'll
    say, 'I'll go back to my first husband,
        for then I was better off than now.'
⁸ But she did not know that it was I who gave her the grain, wine, and oil. I increased
her silver and gold, but they used it for Baal *worship*.

⁹ "Therefore I will
    take away my grain at harvest time,ᵃ
    take away my new wine at its appointed time, and
    take away my wool and linen for covering her private parts.ᵇ ¹⁰ Now I'll
    expose her wanton lust before the eyes of *all* her lovers.
        No one will rescue her from my hand. ¹¹ I'll
    put an end to all her joy,
        feasting, new moon festivals, Sabbaths, and all her appointed festivals;
        ¹² devastate her vines and fig trees
            about which she said, 'These are my *prostitution* wages, which my lovers
            have given me.'
        I'll make them *as useless* as a thicket, and wild animals will eat them.
¹³ Now I will
    punish her for all the days she
        burned incense to the Baals,
        adorned herself with her rings and *other* jewelry, and
        went after her lovers
        but forgot me," declares the LORD.

---

a Literally, "in its season."
b Literally, "her nakedness."

¹⁴ "Therefore, look!
     I am wooing her.
     I will take her to the wilderness and speak *tenderly* to her heart.
  ¹⁵ I will give her her vineyards from there and the Valley of Achor (*e.g.*, Valley of Trouble) for a door of hope.
     She'll respond[a] there like in her younger days, like the day when she came up from Egypt. ¹⁶ On that day," declares the Lord, "she'll call me 'my husband' and no longer call me 'my master.'[b]
  ¹⁷ I will remove the names of the Baals from her mouth,
     and their names will no longer be remembered.[c]
  ¹⁸ I will make a covenant *of peace* with them on that day,
     with the wild animals, the birds in the sky, and things that creep along the ground.
     I'll abolish the bow, sword, and battle from the earth and make them lie down in safety.
¹⁹⁻²⁰ I will betroth you to me forever, betroth you to me in
     – righteousness,   – loyal love,
     – justice,   – compassion, and I'll betroth you to me in
                              – faithfulness.

     And you will know the Lord.

  ²¹ "I will respond on that day," declares the Lord.
     "I'll respond to the sky's *cry for clouds*, and
     it'll respond to the earth's *cry for rain*.
  ²² The earth will respond to the grain, new wine, and oil, and they'll respond *with the cry* 'Jezreel' (*i.e.*, God sows).

  ²³ "I will sow *my people* for myself in the land,[d] and
     I'll have compassion on *the one called* Lo-Ruhamah.
        I'll say to *those called* Not My People, 'You are my people,'
        and she will say, 'You are my God.'"

Hosea **3**

The Lord Loves Israel in Spite of Her Adultery

¹ The Lord said to me,
     "Go again and love *your* wife,
        who is adulterous and loved by *another* lover.
     Go,
        like the Lord who loves the Israelites while they are turning toward other gods and loving the *sacred* raisin cakes."[e]

---

a   Or "will sing."
b   Hebrew: *Baali*, which means "my master" but is also the name of an idol.
c   Literally, "and they shall no longer be remembered by name."
d   Or "I'll sow her as my own in the land."
e   Raisin cakes were used in pagan worship.

^{2} So I bought her for myself for fifteen pieces of silver and ten bushels^a of barley. ^{3} I said to her,

"You shall stay with me for a long time.^{b} You must not engage in prostitution or sleep with a man, and I'll behave similarly toward you."^{c}

^{4} For the Israelites will live for a long time without a king or prince, sacrifice or sacred stone, ephod^d or household gods. ^{5} Afterward the Israelites will return and seek the Lord their God and David their king. They'll tremble before the Lord and his goodness in the last days.

4 Hosea

God's Dispute with Northern Israel

^{1} Listen to the word of the Lord, O *Northern* Israelites!

For the Lord has a dispute with those who live in the land.
"There is
no truth,^{e}
no loyal love,
nor knowledge of God in the land.
^{2} *Rather,*
there is cursing, deceit, murder, robbery, and adultery.
They break forth *on the land*, and *acts of* bloodshed pile up.^{f}
^{3} Therefore
the land mourns *in drought*, and all who live in the land waste away.
The wild animals, the birds in the sky, and even the fish in the sea disappear."

^{4} *To the priests the Lord says,*
"Let not one of you struggle *with another*; no one rebuke another.
My disagreement is with you priests.^{g}

^{5} "You'll stumble by day, and the *false* prophet will stumble with you at night.
I'll destroy your mother.

^{6} "My people are destroyed for lack of knowledge.
You have rejected knowledge,
so I have rejected you from being my priests.
You have forgotten the instruction of your God,
so I too will forget your children.
^{7} The more they multiplied, the more they sinned against me.^{h}
I'll turn their glory into shame.^{i}

---

a Literally, "fifteen *shekels* and a homer and a lethek."
b Literally, "for many days."
c Literally, "and also I for you." This completed God's use of Hosea's family as a metaphor for faithless Israel's return to faithfulness.
d "Ephod": a closely fitted embroidered outer vest used in worship. See Exodus 28:4–14.
e Or "no faithfulness."
f Literally, "and bloodshed reaches bloodshed."
g Or "Your people are the same as who contend with a priest."
h Literally, "As they multiplied, thus they sinned against me."
i Masoretic text; another ancient tradition reads, "They have turned my glory into shame."

⁸ They feed on my people's sin and approve of their iniquity.ᵃ
  ⁹ "So it'll be the same for the people as for the priests.ᵇ I'll punish them
    for their ways and repay them for their deeds.
  ¹⁰ "They'll eat but not be satisfied.
    They'll be promiscuous but not increase in number,ᶜ
      for they have stopped obeying the LORD.
      ¹¹ Prostitution, old wine, and new wineᵈ take away my people's
        understanding.ᵉ
      ¹² They consult their wooden idol, and their *diviner's* wand
        informs them,
          for a spirit of prostitution has made them wander.
        They have engaged in prostitution, instead of *loving* their God.
      ¹³ They offer sacrifices *to idols* on the mountaintops and burn
        incense on the hills,
        under oak, poplar, and terebinth, for their shade is pleasant.
        Therefore your daughters will be whores, and your brides will
        commit adultery.
          ¹⁴ But I won't punish your daughters for prostitution nor your
            brides for adultery,
              because *the men* themselves go off with prostitutes and
              sacrifice with cult prostitutes.
      A people that does not understand will be ruined!

¹⁵ "Though you, *Northern* Israel, engage in prostitution,
    O Judah, do not become guilty *too*!
    Do not go to *worship at* Gilgal nor go up to Beth Aven.
    Do not swear 'As the LORD lives' *there*.

¹⁶ "*Northern* Israel is stubborn like a heifer is stubborn.
    Can the LORD now shepherd them like a lamb in a large field?
¹⁷ Ephraim is allied with idols. Leave him alone.
  ¹⁸ Their beer is gone;
    they engage in promiscuity;
    their leadersᶠ love dishonor.
¹⁹ A whirlwind wraps them in its wings,
  and they'll be ashamed because of their sacrifices.

a   Literally, "and to their iniquity you lift up your soul."
b   Literally, "So it'll be: like people, like priest."
c   Literally, "be filled with prostitution but not break forth."
d   "New wine": freshly pressed grapes, not fully fermented.
e   Literally, "people's heart."
f   Literally, "their shields."

5 *Hosea*

Judgment Against Northern Israel and Judah

¹ "Listen to this, priests.
Pay attention, *northern* Israelites.
Incline your ear, royal household,
> for the judgment is for you.
>> *For by worshiping*
>>> at Mizpah, you have been a trap *for others*.
>>> At Tabor you have spread a net.
>> ² The rebels are knee-deep in slaughter.
I will discipline all of them.

³ "I know Ephraim, and *Northern* Israel is not hidden from me. For now you have engaged in prostitution, Ephraim, and *Northern* Israel is defiled.

⁴ "Their evil deeds won't permit them to return to their God, for a spirit of prostitution is among them, and they do not know the Lord. ⁵ Israel's pride testifies against them.[a] *Northern* Israel and Ephraim will stumble in their iniquity, and Judah will also stumble with them. ⁶ They come with their sheep and their cattle to seek the Lord, but they will not find him. He has withdrawn from them. ⁷ They have committed treachery against the Lord, for they have given birth to illegitimate children. Now the new moon will devour them along with their fields.

⁸ "Sound the ram's horn in Gibeah and the trumpet in Ramah!
Shout an alarm in Beth Aven and afterward in Benjamin!
> ⁹ Ephraim will be a desolation on the day of rebuke.
> I'll make the truth known among the tribes of *all* Israel;
>> ¹⁰ the princes of Judah have become like those who move boundary stones.[b]
> I'll pour out my wrath on them like water.
> ¹¹ Ephraim is oppressed and crushed under *my* judgment,
>> for he was intent on following after idols.[c]

¹² "I will be like a moth to Ephraim and rottenness to Judah.
¹³ "When Ephraim saw his illness, and Judah *saw* his wound,
> Ephraim went to Assyria *for help* and sent *messengers* to the great king.[d]
> But he is unable to cure you or heal your wound.
>> ¹⁴ For I'll be like a lion to Ephraim, a young lion to the house of Judah.
>> I will tear *the prey* and leave;
>> I will take away, and there will be no one to rescue. ¹⁵ Then
>> I'll go and return to my place until they recognize their guilt and
>> seek my face.

"When they are afflicted, they will seek me fervently."

---

a   Literally, "The pride of Israel answers to their face."

b   To move a boundary stone was a serious offense, because it damaged the integrity of God's apportionment of the land to Israel and the livelihood of those whose land had been reduced. See Deuteronomy 19:14; 27:17.

c   The Hebrew after "intent on" is uncertain.

d   Or "to King Jareb," which translates as "King Great." But there is no archeological evidence of a King Jareb.

A Call to Repentance

¹ Come, let us return to the Lord;
   for

      he has torn us *to pieces*, but he will heal us.
      He has struck, but he will bandage *our wounds*.
² He will revive us after two days;ᵃ
   on the third day he will raise us up, and we'll live before him.
³ Let's recognize *the truth*.
  Let's pursue the knowledge of the Lord.

      His appearance will be as sure as the dawn.
      He'll come upon us like rain, like the spring rain that waters the earth.

Israel and Judah Remain Unrepentant

⁴ *The Lord says,*
   "What will I do with you, O Ephraim?
   What will I do with you, O Judah?

      Your loyal love is like a morning mist, like dew that disappears early *in the morning*.
   ⁵ Therefore
      I have cut you down by *the mouth of* the prophets;
      I have slain you by the words from my mouth, and
      judgments on you are like light that shines.
   ⁶ For
      I delight in loyal love, not sacrifice, and in
      the knowledge of God rather than burnt offerings.
   ⁷ But
      they are like men who have brokenᵇ a covenant.
      They committed treachery against me there.
       ⁸ Gilead is the city of evildoers with bloody footprints.
       ⁹ A band of priests is like a band of raiders;
            they commit murder on the way to Shechem;
            they carry out wicked schemes.

¹⁰ "In the house of Israel I have seen a horrible thing:
      Ephraim engaged in prostitution there;
      Israel is defiled.

¹¹ "*Regardless,*
      Judah, a harvest is also appointed for you,
         when I bring back the captives of my people.

---

a Literally, "from days," meaning an unspecified short period.
b Or "like Adam, who transgressed."

7 Hosea

Israel's Sin Exposed

1 "When I heal Israel,
   I will expose Ephraim's iniquity and the evil deeds of Samaria,
      for they have practiced deception.
         The thief goes inside *to steal*, and bandits strip *victims* outside.

2 "They do not consider in their hearts that
      I remember all their evil deeds.
      Now their evil deeds surround them;
      they are right in front of my face.
3 They make the king rejoice when they commit[a] wickedness, and
   they make the princes *rejoice* when they practice deception.
4 All of them are adulterers,
      continuing on like an oven the baker does not need to stoke[b] from the
      kneading of the dough until it rises.[c]

5 "On our king's day *of revelry*,
      princes become weak, inflamed with wine;
      the king joins hands with scoffers,
         6 for their hearts lie in wait like the oven *waits to roast*;
         every night their anger smolders,
            only to awaken in the morning, burning like a flaming fire.
      7 All of them flare like an oven and consume their judges;
      all of their kings fall; none of them call on me.

Israel Relies on Other Nations Instead of God

8 "Ephraim mixes himself among the nations;
   Ephraim has become *as worthless as* a half-baked cake.[d]
      9 Foreigners devour his strength, but he is unaware.
      Gray hairs are sprinkled upon him, but he does not notice.
10 "Israel's pride testifies against them. Yet *despite all this*,
      they have not returned to the LORD their God,
      nor have they sought him despite all of this.
11 Ephraim has become like a silly dove—
      without sense, calling out *first* to Egypt and then going to Assyria *for help*!
         12 Whenever they go,
            I'll spread my net over them;
            I'll bring them down like a bird of the sky;
            I'll catch them when I hear them flock together.[e]

---

a   Literally, "rejoice with." And "when they practice" in the next line.
b   Literally, "the baker ceases to stoke."
c   Literally, "until it is leavened."
d   Literally, "unturned cake."
e   Or "I'll chastise them according to the report to their congregation."

¹³ "Woe to them,

> for they have wandered away from me;
>> destruction is *coming* to them,
>> for they have rebelled against me.
I would redeem them,
but
> they speak lies about me.
> ¹⁴ They have not cried out to me with their hearts when they wail on their beds.
>> *Instead*, they slash themselves for the sake of grain and wine.^a
> They turn away from me.
¹⁵ I trained and strengthened their arms,
> but they plot evil against me.
¹⁶ They return *but* not upward.
> They are like a faulty bow.
> Their princes will fall by the sword because of their insolent tongues.
>> For this they'll be ridiculed in Egypt.

Hosea **8**

Israel Trusts in Idols Instead of God

¹ "*Raise* the trumpet to your mouth, *Hosea*.
Like an eagle *the enemy will come* against the temple,
> for Israel broke my covenant and rebelled against my instruction.

² "They cry out to me, 'We, Israel, know you—*each crying out*, "My God!'
³ But

> Israel has rejected what is good,
>> so the enemy pursues them.
> ⁴ They crowned kings
>> but not *with advice* from me;
> they appointed princes
>> but I didn't know them.
> They made idols for themselves from their silver and gold,
>> *leading to* their own destruction.

⁵ "I have rejected your *golden* calf, O Samaria!
My anger burns against them.
How long will they be incapable of innocence?
> ⁶ For it is from Israel, made by *Israeli* craftsmen, but it is not a god.
> It'll be broken to bits,^b that calf of Samaria.
> ⁷ For they'll sow the wind and reap the whirlwind.
>> The standing grain has no heads; it'll produce no flour;
>>> if it did produce, foreigners would consume it.

---

a "Slash themselves" refers to a pagan worship practice (see 1 Kings 18:28). Or "they assemble themselves for grain and wine."

b The Hebrew for this phrase is uncertain.

⁸ "Israel has been consumed;
  now they are among the nations like an unwanted pot.^a
    ⁹ For they went up to Assyria.
      Like a wild donkey on its own, Ephraim has paid for lovers.
¹⁰ Even though they have paid *for allies* among the nations,
    now I'll gather them up *for judgment*;
    they'll begin to waste away under the *tax* burden of the mighty king.
      ¹¹ For Ephraim has multiplied altars *for sacrifices* for sin;
        but they have become altars for sinning!
      ¹² I wrote for them myriads^b of great things—my law—
        but they are regarded as something strange.

      ¹³ Though they offer sacrifices *and* eat the meat,
        the Lord does not accept them.
      Now he will remember their iniquity and punish their sins;
        they'll return to Egypt.

¹⁴ Israel has forgotten his Creator;
    he has built palaces.
  Judah has multiplied fortified cities,
    so I'll send fire upon their cities;
    it will devour their citadels."^c

9 *Hosea*

Punishment Is Coming for Israel

¹ Do not be joyful, Israel;
  do not cry out for joy like the peoples,
    for you have engaged in prostitution, *turning* away from your God.
    You've earned prostitutes' wages^d on every threshing floor.
  ² The threshing floor and winepress won't feed the people of Israel,^e and
    this year's wine vintage^f will fail them.
  ³ They won't remain in the Lord's land;
    Ephraim will return to Egypt,
    and they will eat unclean *food* in Assyria.
  ⁴ They won't pour out wine as drink offerings to the Lord.
    Their sacrifices won't please him.

---

a Literally, "like a pot in which nobody delights."
b Literally, "ten thousand," an expression commonly used figuratively.
c Or "its palatial buildings."
d Literally, "made love for hire."
e Literally, "not feed them."
f Literally, "and this year's new wine."

All their food will be like mourners' bread to them;
　　anyone who eats it will be defiled,
　　　　for their food is only for their appetites.
　　It won't enter the house of the Lord.
　⁵ So what will you do on a festival day or on the Lord's feast day?

⁶ For look! *Though* they escape from destruction,
　　Egypt will gather them; Memphis will bury them.
　　Weeds will grow up around*ᵃ* their treasures of silver;
　　thorns will be in their tents.

⁷ Let Israel know this:
　　The days of punishment have come;
　　the days of recompense have arrived!

　The prophet is *thought* a fool, and the inspired one insane,
　　because of the multitude of your iniquities and
　　because your hostility is so vast.
⁸ The prophet, along with my God, was a watchman over Ephraim;
　　but now a bird-catcher's trap is on all his paths,
　　and there is *nothing but* hostility *toward him* in the house of his God.
⁹ They have plunged into corruption like in the days of Gibeah.*ᵇ*
God will remember their iniquity and punish their sins.

¹⁰ *God says,*
　　"I found Israel like grapes in the wilderness;
　　　　you were like the firstfruits of a fig tree in its first *season.*
　　I took notice of your ancestors.
　　　　They came to Baal Peor and dedicated themselves to a shameful *idol;*
　　　　they became despicable like the thing they loved.

　¹¹ "As for Ephraim, their glory will fly away like a bird:
　　　　no birth, no pregnancy, no conception.
　　　¹² If they should rear their children, I'll take every one of them.*ᶜ*
　　They'll have woe when I turn away from them!
　¹³ Ephraim, as I have seen, is like Tyre, planted in a meadow;
　　　　but Ephraim will bring their children out to the slayer."

¹⁴ *Hosea answers,*
　　"Give them, O Lord; what will you give them?
　　Give them
　　　　a miscarrying womb and
　　　　shriveled breasts."

---

a　Literally, "will possess."
b　See Judges 19:16–30.
c　Literally, "I'll bereave them of every one." "Bereave": to be deprived of a loved one, especially through their death.

11

¹⁵ *God continues,*

"All their evil was at Gilgal,
so I hated them there.
Because of their wicked deeds,
I'll drive them out of my temple.
I won't love them any longer—
all their princes are rebels.
¹⁶ Ephraim has been struck; their roots are dry; they have borne no fruit.
Though they bear children, I'll slay the precious *fruit* of their womb."

¹⁷ *And Hosea mourns,*

"My God will reject them,
for they have not listened to him;
they'll become wanderers among the nations."

10 *Hosea*

Israel Will Reap Captivity for Its Sins

¹ Israel is a lush vine that yields fruit for itself,
but he has multiplied his altars like the vast amount of his fruit.
As his land prospered, so he adorned his sacred pillars.
² The hearts *of the people* are divided; now they must bear their guilt.
The Lord will break up their altars and destroy their sacred pillars.

³ Surely now they are saying,

"We have no king, for we do not fear the Lord.
As for the king, what can he do for us?"
⁴ They speak *false* words,
swear false oaths, and
make *false* covenants.
Judgment will shoot up like a poisonous plant in the furrows of a field.

⁵ Those who live in Samaria will fear for the *golden* calf at Beth Aven.
Its people will mourn for it,
as will its idolatrous priests who used to rejoice over it,
for its splendor has been taken from them into exile.
⁶ It will be brought to Assyria as tribute to the great king;
Ephraim will be seized with shame, and
Israel will be ashamed of its plan.

⁷ Samaria will be destroyed;
her king will be like a broken twig on the surface of the water.
⁸ The high-place shrines of wickedness^a and sin in Israel will be destroyed.
Thorns and thistles will grow up over their altars.
The people will call^b to the mountains, "Cover us!"
And to the heights, "Fall on us!"

---

a   Or "high places of Aven." The Hebrew word *aven* translates as "wickedness."
b   Literally, "They will say."

⁹ *The Lord says,*

"Since the days of Gibeah you have sinned, O Israel;
there you have remained.*ᵃ*
Won't war overtake the evildoers*ᵇ* at Gibeah?
¹⁰ I will chastise them when I please;
nations will be gathered against them to put them in bonds*ᶜ* for their
double sin.

¹¹ "Ephraim is a trained heifer that loves to thresh,
but I will harness*ᵈ* her lovely neck *with a yoke.*
I'll harness Ephraim,
Judah will plow, and
Jacob must harrow for himself.*ᵉ*

¹² "Sow righteousness for yourselves;
reap in lovingkindness.*ᶠ*
Break up your fallow*ᵍ* ground,
for the time has come to seek the LORD until he comes and showers
righteousness upon you.

¹³ "You have plowed wickedness and reaped evil;
you have eaten the fruit of deception,
for you trusted in your own way and in your numerous warriors.
¹⁴ Therefore
an uproar will arise against your people, and
all your fortified cities will be destroyed
like Shalman destroyed Beth Arbel*ʰ* on the day of battle,
when mothers were dashed to pieces with *their* children.
¹⁵ So it will be done to you, Bethel, because of your great wickedness.
The king of Israel will be utterly destroyed at dawn."

Hosea **11**

God's Enduring Love for Israel

¹ *The Lord continues,*

"When Israel was a youth I loved him, and I called my son out of Egypt.
² But the more the prophets*ⁱ* called them,
the more they went away from them,
sacrificing to the Baals and burning incense to idols.

---

a Literally, "there you stood."
b Literally, "the sons of evil" or "of injustice."
c Or "when they are bound."
d Literally, "I will pass over."
e "Harrow": to break up the clods and smooth out plowed ground—a metaphor for a hardened heart.
f It is unclear whether this means you will reap (i.e., receive) lovingkindness or you are to give it as you reap.
g "Fallow ground": uncultivated, unplowed.
h Beth Arbel is an unknown location. Shalman may be a reference to Shalmanezer III, king of Assyria.
i Literally, "they."

³ "It was I who taught Ephraim to walk;
   I took them in my arms, but they did not know that I healed them.
⁴ I led them with cords of human *kindness*, with bonds of love;
      to them I was like one who lifts a yoke from their jaws;
   I bent down to feed them.
⁵ But because they refuse to repent,
      they won't return to Egypt, and
      won't Assyria be their king?
      ⁶ The sword will whirl in their cities and put an end to the bars of their *city* gates;
      it will devour *them* because of their own plans.
⁷ My people are bent on turning from me;
   though they call out to the Most High, none of them exalt him.

⁸ "How can I give you up, Ephraim? Or hand you over, O Israel?
   How can I make you like Admah or put you *to an end* like Zeboiim?*ᵃ*
   I've had a change of heart;*ᵇ* my compassion is stirred up!
      ⁹ I won't carry out my fierce anger;
      I won't destroy Ephraim,
         for I am God, not a human.
      I am the Holy One in your midst;
      I won't come in wrath.*ᶜ*

¹⁰ "They will follow the LORD;
      he'll roar like a lion.
   When he roars,
      his children will come trembling from the west.
      ¹¹ They'll come trembling like a bird from Egypt and like a dove from
      Assyria;
   I will settle them in their houses," declares the LORD.

¹² Ephraim has surrounded me with lies and the people of Israel with deception;
   Judah is still roaming away from God, the faithful Holy One.

12 Hosea

God Pleads with Israel to Return
¹ Ephraim feeds on the wind and pursues the east wind all day long.
   He multiplies lies and violence, and
   he makes a treaty with Assyria and will bring oil *as tribute* to Egypt.

² The LORD has a lawsuit against Judah, to punish Jacob for his ways,
   and he will repay him for his deeds.
      ³ He grabbed his brother's heel in the womb,*ᵈ* and

---

a Admah and Zeboiim were destroyed in the "Lord's anger." See Deuteronomy 29:23.
b Literally, "My heart is overturned upon me."
c Or "I won't come into a city."
d See Genesis 25:26.

he strove with God when he was mature.
⁴ He strove with the angel and prevailed;
he wept and begged for his favor.ᵃ
He found God at Bethel and spoke with him there.
⁵ The Lᴏʀᴅ God of Armies, the Lᴏʀᴅ is his name.

⁶ As for you,
return to your God.
Guard loyal love and justice;
hope inᵇ your God always.

⁷ A merchant who has dishonest scales in his hands is one who loves to oppress.
⁸ *Like him*, Ephraim said,
"How I have become rich! I have found wealth for myself!
In all my labors they won't find iniquity, which is sin in me."

⁹ *The Lord says*,
"I have been the Lᴏʀᴅ your God since the land of Egypt;
I will again make you live in tents, as in the days of the Festival of Shelters.ᶜ
¹⁰ I spoke to the prophets, and I multiplied visions;
I spoke in riddles by the prophets.

¹¹ Is there iniquity in Gilead?
Surely its people are worthless!
They sacrifice bulls in Gilgal;
indeed, their altars will be like piles of rocks on a plowed field."

¹² Jacob fled to Aram, and Israel worked for a wife.ᵈ
He guarded *sheep to pay* for her.ᵉ
¹³ The Lᴏʀᴅ brought Israel up from Egypt by a prophet,
and by a prophet he was guarded.
¹⁴ Ephraim has provoked *him* to bitter anger.
The Lord will
leave the guilt for his bloodshed on him and
repay him for their sins.ᶠ

Hosea 13

God's Judgment over Israel's Continuing Sin

¹ When Ephraim spoke, there was trembling.
He was exaltedᵍ in Israel;
then he became guilty through Baal *worship* and died.

---

a   See Genesis 32:24–28.
b   Or "wait on."
c   Literally, "like the days of an appointed festival."
d   See Genesis 28:2–5.
e   See Genesis 29.
f   Literally, "and bring his reproach back upon him."
g   Or "exalted himself."

² Now they sin more and more.

> They are making molten images for themselves,
>> idols from their silver, with their skill,
>> all of them the work of artisans.
> It is said about them,
>> "They offer human sacrifices!
>> They kiss calf-idols!"

³ Therefore they will be

> like the morning mist,
> like dew that vanishes early,
> like chaff that is driven away from the threshing floor, or
> like smoke from a chimney.

⁴ "I am the Lord your God since Egypt;

> you shall know no gods except me; there is no savior but me.

⁵ I knew you in the wilderness, in a land of drought.

> ⁶ But as *they fed on* their pasture, they became satisfied;
> they became satisfied and then proud.^{*a*}
>> As a result, they forgot me. ⁷ So

I will be like a young lion to them.

I will lie in wait for them like a leopard on the road.

⁸ I will meet them like a she-bear robbed of her cubs.

> I'll rip open their chests^{*b*} and devour them there
>> like a lioness, like a wild beast would tear them apart.

⁹ Being against me, against your helper, leads to^{*c*} your destruction, Israel.

¹⁰ "So where is your king that he may save you in all your cities, and *where are* the judges of whom you requested, 'Give me a king and princes'?^{*d*} ¹¹ In my anger I gave you a king, and I took him away in my wrath.

¹² "Ephraim's iniquity is bound up; his sin is stored up.

¹³ Pangs like those of a woman in childbirth come upon him.

> He is not a wise son.
> At the time to be born he hangs back^{*e*} at the opening of the womb.

¹⁴ "I will ransom them from the power of the grave;

I will redeem them from death.

> O Death, where are your plagues?
> O Grave, where is your sting?

Compassion will be hidden from my sight.

> ¹⁵ Even though Ephraim^{*f*} flourishes among his brothers,
> An east wind from the Lord will come up from the wilderness, and

---

a Literally, "and then lifted up their heart."
b Literally, "the enclosure of their heart."
c Literally, "It is."
d See 1 Samuel 8:5; 19.
e Literally, "For time he does not stand."
f Literally, "though he."

it'll parch his spring; it'll dry up his well.
　　It will plunder his treasury of every precious thing.
16 Samaria is guilty, for she has rebelled against her God.
　　Her people will fall by the sword—little ones will be dashed to pieces;
　　pregnant women will be split open."

Hosea **14**

God's Promise of Restoration

1 Return, O Israel, to the LORD your God,
　　for you have stumbled in your iniquity.
2 Take words *of repentance* with you and
　return to the LORD.
　Say to him,
　　　"Forgive*ᵃ* all our iniquity and receive us graciously,
　　　　that we may offer you praise.*ᵇ*
　　3 Assyria won't save us;
　　　we won't ride on horses.
　　We will no longer say, 'Our god' to what our hands make.*ᶜ*
　　　because in you the orphan finds compassion."

4 *The Lord says,*
　　　"I will heal their waywardness; I'll love them freely,
　　　　for my anger has turned from them.
　　5 I will be like the dew to Israel;
　　　he'll blossom like the lily.
　　He'll put down roots like *the cedars of* Lebanon.
　　　6 His young shoots will sprout;
　　　　his splendor will be like an olive tree, and
　　　　his fragrance will be like *the cedars of* Lebanon.
　　　　7 Those who live in his shadow will again flourish like the grain;*ᵈ*
　　　　　they'll blossom like the vine.
　　Israel's fame will be like the wine of Lebanon.

　　8 "O Ephraim, how much more do I have to put up with*ᵉ your* idols?
　　　It is I who answers *your prayers* and watches over you.
　　　I am like a flourishing juniper;
　　　your fruit is found in me."

9 Whoever is wise—understand these things.
　Whoever is discerning—know them.
　　For the ways of the LORD are upright;
　　　the righteous walk in them,
　　　but transgressors stumble in them.

---

a　Literally, "Take away" or "lift up."
b　Literally, "may offer you the fruit of our lips."
c　Literally, "to the work of our hands."
d　Or "will cause grain to flourish."
e　Literally, "what do I have to do with."

Joel

1 *Joel*

¹ The word of the Lord that came to Joel son of Pethuel.

A Plague of Locusts

² Listen to this, you elders! Give ear, everyone who lives in the land!
   Has this *ever* happened in your days or in the days of your ancestors?
   ³ Tell your children about it, and *let* your children *tell it to* theirs, and their children to the next generation.
      ⁴ What the locust swarm has left, the great locusts have eaten;
      what the great locusts have left, the young locusts have eaten;
      what the young locusts have left, even more locusts have eaten.ᵃ

⁵ Wake up, you drunkards, and weep.
Wail, all who drink wine,
   because of the new wine takenᵇ from your lips.
      ⁶ For a nation has risen up against my land.
      They are mighty and innumerable.
      They have the teeth of a lion and the jaws of a lioness.
         ⁷ They have made my vine desolate and my fig tree a stump.
            They completely stripped it *of bark* and threw it away, leaving the branches white.

⁸ Mourn like a virgin dressed in sackcloth for the husband she married while she was young.
   ⁹ The grain offering and drink offering are cut off from the temple of the Lord.
   The priests, those who minister to the Lord, mourn.
      ¹⁰ The fields are ruined; the land mourns,
      for
         the grain is ruined,
         the new wine *vintage* is dried up, and
         the olive oil is gone.ᶜ

¹¹ Be ashamed, O plowmen! Wail, you vinedressers,
   for the wheat and barley, for the harvest of the field has perished!
      ¹² The vine is dried up;
      the fig tree is withered;
      the pomegranate, date palm, and apple tree—all the trees in the field—have dried up.
   For everyone's joy has withered away.

¹³ Put on *sackcloth* and sound the lament, O priests;
wail, O ministers of the altar!

---

a   The exact difference in meanings of the four Hebrew terms for locusts in this verse is unknown. Other possible modifiers include creeping, cutting, destroying, devouring, hopping, stripping, and swarming.
b   Literally, "cut off."
c   Literally, "has wasted away."

Come and spend the night in sackcloth, ministers of my God,
for the grain offering and drink offering are withheld from the house of your God.
¹⁴ Consecrate a fast; proclaim a solemn assembly;
gather to the temple of the LORD your God
the elders *and*
everyone who lives in the land, and
cry out to the LORD.

¹⁵ Alas for that day, for the day of the LORD is near!
It is coming as destruction from the Almighty.
¹⁶ Isn't it before our eyes?
Hasn't food been cut off before our eyes—joy and gladness from the temple of
our God?
¹⁷ The seeds are shriveled beneath clods *of dirt.ᵃ*
The storehouses are desolate; the barns are broken down,
because the grain has dried up.
¹⁸ How the livestock groan! The herds of cattle mill about,
for there is no pasture for them; the flocks of sheep suffer as well.

¹⁹ I call out to you, O LORD,
for fire has devoured the grazing areas in the wilderness,
and flames have burned up all the trees in the field.
²⁰ Even the livestock in the field pant for you,
for the streams of water have dried up,
and fire has devoured the grazing areas in the wilderness.

Joel 2

The Day of the Lord Described

¹ Sound the trumpet in Zion!
Sound the alarm on my holy mountain!
Let everyone who lives in the land tremble,
for the day of the LORD is coming.
It is near—
² a day of darkness and gloom, a day of clouds and blackness.
Like the dawn*ing light* spreads over the mountains, an army great and
numerous *comes.*
There has never been *anything* like it before, and after it there will never
be *anything like it* again for generation after generation.
³ A fire devours before them, and flames lick up behind them.
The land is like the garden of Eden before them,
but behind them it is a desolate wilderness.
Nothing escapes them.
⁴ Their appearance is like that of horses;
they charge on like war horses.

---

a   The Hebrew for this line is uncertain.

⁵ Like the sound of chariots, they skip about on the mountaintops,
  like the sound of a blazing fire devouring stubble,
  like a mighty army deployed for battle.
⁶ Peoples are in anguish before them; every face turns pale.

⁷ They run like warriors; like men of war they scale walls.
  Each one marches *straight* on his way; they do not change direction.ᵃ
⁸ They do not jostle one another;
  each goes straight ahead.ᵇ
  They plunge through the weapons *launched against them* and do not stop.
⁹ They rush into the city and run along the wall;
  they come up to houses and enter through the windows like thieves.

¹⁰ The land trembles before them; the heavens shake.
  The sun and moon are darkened; the stars lose their luster.

¹¹ The Lᴏʀᴅ lifts his voice before his army,
    for his camp is very large;
    for greatᶜ are they who execute his word.
The day of the Lᴏʀᴅ is great and awesome indeed; who can endure it?

The Lord's Call to Repentance

¹² "Even now," declares the Lᴏʀᴅ,
  "Return to me
    with all your hearts,
    with fasting, weeping, and mourning."
 ¹³ Rend your hearts, not your garments.
  Return to the Lᴏʀᴅ your God,
  for he is
    gracious and merciful,
    slow to anger,ᵈ and
    abundant in loyal love.
  He relents from disaster.
 ¹⁴ Who knows whether he'll turn and relent and leave behind a blessing,
    a grain offering and drink offering for the Lᴏʀᴅ your God?

¹⁵ Sound the trumpet in Zion!
 Consecrate a fast;
 proclaim a solemn assembly!
  ¹⁶ Assemble the people;
    consecrate the congregation;
    gather the elders;
    gather even the little children and those who still nurse.ᵉ

---

a Literally, "not turn from their path."
b Literally, "goes in his path."
c Whether "great" refers to numbers or strength is unclear.
d Literally, "long of nostrils."
e Literally, "those who suck the breasts."

20

Let the groom come out of his room and the bride from her chamber.

[17] Let the priests, those who minister to the Lord,

weep between the porch and the altar.

Let them say,

"O Lord, spare your people.

Do not give your inheritance over to disgrace, *to become* a byword among the nations.

Why should *unbelieving foreigners* say[a] among the peoples, 'Where is their God?'"

Blessings for Israel

[18] The Lord will be jealous for his land;

he will take pity on his people.

[19] The Lord will say to his people,

"Look! I'm sending you grain, wine, and oil,

and you'll *eat them and* be satisfied by them.

I will no longer make you an object of scorn among the nations.

[20] I'll take the northern *army* far away from you.

I'll drive it into a waterless, desolate land—

its vanguard into the Dead Sea and its rear guard into the Mediterranean sea.[b]

Its stench will rise, and its reek will go up."

Surely, he has done great things!

[21] Do not fear, O land; rejoice and shout for joy,

for the Lord has done great things!

[22] Do not fear, livestock in the field,

for the grazing places in the wilderness will sprout grass.

Trees will *again* bear their fruit;

the fig tree and vine will give their produce.[c]

[23] People of Zion, shout for joy! Rejoice in the Lord your God,

for he has given you the autumn rains for your vindication.[d]

He has poured down abundant rain for you, autumn rain and spring rain,[e] as before.

[24] The threshing floors will be full of grain;

the vats will overflow with new wine and oil.

[25] *The Lord says,*

"I will repay you for the years the locust swarm has eaten—

the great locust, the young locust, and the other locusts,

my great army that I sent against you.

---

a   Literally, "they say."

b   Literally, "their faces into the eastern sea and their end into the western sea."

c   Literally, "their strength."

d   Literally, "for righteousness."

e   Literally, "former rain" or "early rain" and "latter rain."

²⁶ You will have plenty to eat, and you will be satisfied.
You will praise the name of the Lᴏʀᴅ your God who has done wonderful
things for you.
My people will never be put to shame again forever.
   ²⁷ Then you'll know that I am in Israel's midst;
   I am the Lᴏʀᴅ your God; there is no other!
My people will never *again* be put to shame.

²⁸ "After this,
   I will pour out my Spirit on all people;
   your sons and daughters will prophesy.
   Your elders will dream dreams, and your young men will see visions.
²⁹ And also on *both* the men and the women who serve me,^a I will pour out my
Spirit in those days.
³⁰ I will give signs in the sky and on the earth:
   blood, fire, and billows of smoke.
      ³¹ The sun will be turned into darkness and the moon into blood
         before the coming of the great and awesome day of the Lᴏʀᴅ.
³² All who call on the name of the Lᴏʀᴅ will be saved,
   for there will be deliverance on Mount Zion and in Jerusalem,
just as the Lᴏʀᴅ has promised, and they'll be among the survivors whom the
Lᴏʀᴅ calls.

3 *Joel*

Judgment for the Nations

¹ "Indeed! In those days and at that time, when I bring back the captives of Judah
and Jerusalem,
   ² I'll gather all the nations.
   I'll bring them down to the Valley of Jehoshaphat
      (*i.e.*, Valley of the Lᴏʀᴅ's Judgment), and
   I'll judge them there regarding *their treatment of*
      my people, my inheritance Israel,
         whom they scattered among the nations, and
      my land
         that they divided.
   ³ They have
      cast lots for my people,
      traded a boy for a whore, and
      sold a girl for wine, so they can get drunk!

⁴ "Also,
      what are you to me, Tyre and Sidon and all the regions of Philistia?
      Are you retaliating against me?

---

a   Literally, "On both the menservants and the maidservants."

22

If you retaliate against me, I'll swiftly and speedily return your hit[a] back
on your own heads;

⁵ for you have

taken my silver and gold,

carried off my finest treasures to your temples. ⁶ You have

sold the people of Judah and Jerusalem *as slaves* to the Greeks and
have removed them far away from their territory.

⁷ Indeed! I will

summon them out of the place where you sold them and

return your repayment upon your heads.

⁸ I'll sell your sons and daughters into the hands of the people of Judah,
and they'll sell them to the Sabeans, a distant nation,"[b]

for the Lord has spoken.

⁹ Proclaim this among the nations:

"Prepare for war!

Rouse the warriors!

Let all the men of war arrive *here* and then go up *to fight*.

¹⁰ Beat your plowshares into swords and your pruning hooks into spears.

Let the weakling say, 'I am strong!'"

¹¹ Come quickly,[c] all nations around us, and gather there.

O Lord, bring down your warriors.

¹² *The Lord says,*

"May the nations be roused and come up to the Valley of Jehoshaphat (i.e., of
the Lord's judgment),

for there I'll sit to judge all the surrounding nations.

¹³ Swing the sickle, for the harvest is ripe.

Come, tread *the grapes of their sin*—the winepress is full from the
overflowing vats;

for their wickedness is great."

¹⁴ Multitudes, multitudes in the valley of decision! For the day of the Lord is near
in the valley of decision. ¹⁵ The sun and moon are darkened, and the stars lose
their luster.

More Blessings for the Israelites

¹⁶ The Lord will

roar from Zion and

raise his voice from Jerusalem.

Heaven and earth will tremble.

But the Lord will be

a refuge for his people,

a stronghold for the Israelites.

---

a Literally, "your recompense."
b "Sabeans" were descendants of Sheba (see Genesis 25:3), who lived in the area of today's Yemen.
c Literally, "Assemble and come."

¹⁷ *The Lord says,*
"Then
you will know that I am the L<small>ORD</small> your God,
who dwells on Zion,
my holy mountain.
Jerusalem will be holy; foreigners won't pass through her again.

¹⁸ "On that day,
the mountains will drip with sweet wine;
the hills will run with milk;
all the streams of Judah will flow with water; and
a fountain will come out of the L<small>ORD</small>'s temple to water the Valley of Shittim
(*i.e.,* Valley of Acacia Trees).^{*a*}
¹⁹ Egypt will become a wasteland.
Edom will become a desolate wilderness,
because of the violence they perpetrated on the people of Judah when
they spilled innocent blood in their land.
²⁰ Judah will be inhabited forever and Jerusalem for all generations.

²¹ "I will avenge their blood, *blood* that I have not *yet* avenged,"
for the L<small>ORD</small> dwells in Zion!

---

a   Or "Valley of Acacias."

24

Amos

Part I. Pronouncement of Judgment

¹ The message of Amos, one of the shepherds from Tekoa,
    which he saw concerning Israel in the days of Uzziah king of Judah and
    in the days of Jeroboam son of Jehoash, king of *Northern* Israel, two years
    before the earthquake.

Judgment Is Coming upon Israel's Enemies

² He said,
    "The LORD roars from Zion; he raises his voice from Jerusalem.
    The shepherds' pastures mourn;
    the summit of Mount Carmel is dried up."

³ The LORD says this: "For three sins, even for four, I will not turn back *my wrath*[a] from Damascus
    because they threshed Gilead with sharp iron sledges.[b]
        ⁴ I'll send fire upon the house of Hazael to devour the citadels of Ben-Hadad.[c]
        ⁵ I'll break down the gates[d] of Damascus.
        I'll cut off those who live in the Valley of Aven and the one who holds the
        scepter from the house of Beth Eden.[e]
            The people of Aram will go into exile in Kir," says the LORD.

⁶ The LORD says this: "For three sins, even for four, I will not turn back *my wrath* from Gaza,
    because they deported an entire population and handed them over to Edom.
        ⁷ I'll send fire upon the walls of Gaza, and it'll devour her citadels.
        ⁸ I'll cut off the population of Ashdod and seize the scepter from Ashkelon.
        I'll turn my hand against Ekron,
            and the remnant of the Philistines will perish," says the Lord GOD.

⁹ The LORD says this: "For three sins, even for four, I will not turn back *my wrath* from Tyre,
    because they handed over an entire population to Edom,
    and they did not remember the covenant of brotherhood.
        ¹⁰ I'll send fire upon the walls of Tyre,
            and it'll devour her citadels."

---

a   Or "*its punishment.*" And verses 6, 9, 11, and 13.
b   "Sledge": a tool for separating grain from chaff.
c   Hazael and Ben-Hadad were kings of Damascus.
d   Literally, "the bar."
e   "Beth Eden": a name for Damascus.

¹¹ The LORD says this: "For three sins, even for four, I will not turn back *my wrath* from Edom,

> because he pursued his brother with the sword and showed no*ᵃ* mercy.
> His anger raged continually, and he held onto his wrath unrelentingly.
>> ¹² So I'll send fire upon Teman,
>>> and it'll devour the citadels of Bozrah."

¹³ The LORD says this: "For three sins, even for four, I will not turn back *my wrath* from Ammon,

> because they slashed open the pregnant women of Gilead in order to enlarge their territory.
>> ¹⁴ I'll kindle a fire against the walls of Rabbah,
>>> and it'll devour her citadels amid the war cries on the day of battle and the gale on a stormy day.
>>> ¹⁵ Their king will go into exile, he and his princes together," says the LORD.

2 Amos

¹ The LORD says this: "For three sins, even for four, I will not turn back *my wrath*ᵇ from Moab,

> because he burned the bones of the king of Edom to lime.
>> ² I'll send fire upon Moab.
>> It'll devour the citadels of Kerioth.
>> Moab will die amid tumult, war cries, and the sound of the trumpet.
>> ³ I'll cut off the judge from within her,
>>> and I'll slay all her princes with him," says the LORD.

Judgment Is Coming upon Israel

⁴ The LORD says this: "For three sins, even for four, I will not turn back *my wrath* from Judah,

> because they rejected the instruction of the LORD and did not observe his statutes. Their lies have led them astray, *lies* which their ancestors *also* followed.
>> ⁵ So I'll send fire upon Judah, and it'll devour the citadels of Jerusalem."

⁶ The LORD says this: "For three sins, even for four, I will not turn back *my wrath* from Israel, because

> they sell the righteous for silver and the needy for a pair of sandals.
>> ⁷ They crush the heads of the poor into the dust of the ground, and
> they oppress the humble.*ᶜ*
> A man and his father go in to the *same* girl and so profane my holy name.
>> ⁸ They lie down beside every altar on garments taken in pledge and drink wine taken as fines in the house of their god.

---

a Literally, "and corrupted."
b Or "*its punishment.*" And verses 4 and 6.
c Literally, "the way of the humble they turn aside."

⁹ "Yet I destroyed the Amorite before Israel, though they were as tall as cedars and strong as oaks;

I destroyed their fruit above and their root beneath. ¹⁰ "And I brought you up from Egypt,

led you through the wilderness for forty years to possess the Amorites' land,

¹¹ raised up prophets from your children and Nazirites*a* from your young men.

Isn't this true, O Israelites?" declares the LORD.

¹² But you

made the Nazirites drink wine

and overruled*b* the prophets, saying, 'Do not prophesy!'

¹³ "Listen! I will crush you like a wagon crushes *the ground* when full of sheaves *of wheat.c*

¹⁴ The swift won't escape*d* nor the strong increase their power.

The warrior won't save his life.

¹⁵ The archer won't survive;*e*

the swift of foot won't escape; and

the one who rides a horse won't save his life.

¹⁶ Even the bravest warriors will flee naked on that day," declares the LORD.

Part 2. Prophecies Against Israel

Amos 3

Listen, Israel; Amos Must Prophesy

¹ Listen to this message that the LORD has spoken against you, O Israelites, against the entire family that the LORD brought up from Egypt:

² "I have chosen*f* you alone from all the families on the earth;

therefore I will punish you for all your iniquities."

³ "Do two people walk together unless they have agreed to?

⁴ Does the lion roar in the forest if he has no prey?

Does the young lion lift his voice from his den if he has caught nothing?

⁵ Does a bird fall into a trap on the ground when it has no bait?

Does a trap spring up from the ground when it hasn't caught anything?

⁶ If the trumpet is blown in the city, will the people not tremble?

If there is a disaster in the city, has the LORD not caused it?

⁷ For the Lord GOD does nothing without revealing his plan to his servants the prophets.

---

a "Nazirites": Israelites who took a special vow of holiness. See numbers 6:1-21.
b Literally, "commanded."
c The meaning of the Hebrew for this line is uncertain.
d Literally, "Safety will perish from the swift."
e Literally, "The one who grasps the bow won't stand."
f Literally, "I have known."

^{8} The lion has roared; who is not frightened?
The Lord God speaks; who can fail to prophesy?

^{9} "Proclaim it to the citadels of Ashdod and to the citadels in Egypt;
say,
'Gather on the mountains in Samaria;
look at the great unrest within her and oppressed *people* in her midst.'"

^{10} The Lord declares,
"They do not know how to do what is right, these *people* who store up *their gains from* violence and destruction in their citadels."

^{11} Therefore the Lord God says this:
"An enemy
will surround your land,
pull down your strongholds, and
loot your citadels."

^{12} The Lord says this:
"Just like a shepherd rescues two legs or part of an ear from the lion's mouth, so will the Israelites living in Samaria be rescued—with *only* the corner of a bed or the cover of a couch."

^{13} The Lord God of Armies declares,
"Listen and testify against the family of Jacob.
^{14} For on the day that I punish Israel for its sins,
I'll visit *destruction* on the altars at Bethel.
The horns of the altar will be chopped off and fall to the ground.
^{15} I'll smash the winter house and the summer house.
The houses decorated with ivory^a will disappear,
and many houses^b will come to an end," declares the Lord.

4 Amos

Israel's Guilt and Refusal to Return to God

^{1} Listen to this message, you cows of Bashan,^{c}
who
are *worshiping* on Mount Samaria,
oppress the poor,
crush the needy, and
say to your husbands, "Bring us some drinks!"

^{2} The Lord God has sworn by his holiness,
"Listen! The days are coming upon you when
they will take you away with hooks,
the last of you with fishhooks.
^{3} You'll go out *through* gaps *in the walls*,
each one straight through, and
you'll be thrown out toward Harmon,"^{d} declares the Lord.

---

a Literally, "of ivory."
b Or "and the great houses."
c "Cows of Bashan": Bashan was known for its good grazing grass.
d "Harmon": an unknown location.

⁴ "Come to Bethel and sin—to Gilgal and multiply sin!
Bring your sacrifices in the morning, on the third day your tithes.*ᵃ*
⁵ Offer a sacrifice of thanksgiving with leavened bread, and
announce your freewill offerings;
boast about them,
for this is what you love *to do*, O Israelites," declares the Lord God.

⁶ "Even though
I have given you famine*ᵇ* in all your cities and lack of bread in all your
settlements, yet
you still have not turned to me," declares the Lord.
⁷ *"Even though*
I have also withheld rain from you when it was still three months
from harvesttime;
I gave rain to one city but withheld rain from another city;
I withheld rain from one parcel, and it rained upon another.
The parcel it did not rain upon dried up.
⁸ Two or three cities would stagger up to one city to drink water, but they
would not be satisfied; yet
you have not returned to me," declares the Lord.

⁹ "When your gardens, vineyards, fig trees, and olive trees flourished, locusts
devoured them. But you still have not returned to me," declares the Lord.

¹⁰ "I sent a plague against you like *the one* in Egypt;
I killed your young men with the sword along with your captured horses;
I made the stench of your camp rise up in your nostrils, but
you *still* have not returned to me," declares the Lord.

¹¹ "I overthrew you like when God overthrew Sodom and Gomorrah,
and you were like a burning stick snatched from the fire; but
you *still* have not returned to me," declares the Lord.

¹² "Therefore I will do this to you, O Israel.
Because I will do this to you,
prepare to meet your God, O Israel!
¹³ Note well!
The Maker of the mountains, Creator of the wind,
the one
who tells people what they are thinking,
who turns dawn to darkness,
who treads on the high places of the earth—
the Lord God of Armies is his name!"

---

a   Or "your tithes every three days."
b   Literally, "given you cleanness of teeth."

5 *Amos*

A Lament over Israel

¹ Listen to this message, which I take up as a lament for you, O Israel:
> ² "Virgin Israel has fallen and won't rise again.
> She lies abandoned on her land; there is no one to lift her up."

³ For the Lord God says this to the Israelites:
> "The city that sends out *a force of* a thousand will have *only* a hundred left;
> the one that sends out a hundred will have *only* ten left."

⁴ For the Lord says this to the Israelites:
> "Seek me and live!
> > ⁵ Do not inquire of *the idols at* Bethel.
> > Do not go to Gilgal; do not pass through Beersheba,
> > > for Gilgal will certainly go into exile,
> > > and Bethel will come to be nothing."

⁶ Seek the Lord and live,
> or he'll rush upon the family of Joseph like a wildfire.
> The fire will devour them, and Bethel will have no one to quench it.

⁷ There are those who
> turn justice into bitterness^{*a*} and
> throw righteousness to the ground.

⁸ He who
> made the Pleiades and Orion,^{*b*}
> changes deep darkness into morning,
> darkens day into night,
> calls for the waters of the sea and pours them out on the surface of the earth,
the Lord is his name.
> ⁹ He is the one who rains ruin on the strong
> > so that destruction comes upon a fortified city.

¹⁰ *In Israel,*
> the one who reproves *injustice* at the gate is hated.
> The one who speaks with integrity is abhorred.
> > ¹¹ Therefore since you trample on the poor and tax their grain,
> > > *though* you have built houses out of dressed stone,^{*c*}
> > > > you won't live in them.
> > > Though you have planted lush vineyards,
> > > > you won't drink wine from them.
> > ¹² For I know the multitude of your transgressions, the vast numbers of your sins—
> > > oppressing the righteous,
> > > accepting bribes,
> > > and turning *justice* away *from* the needy in the gate!

---

a   Literally, "into wormwood," an herb with an extraordinarily bitter taste.
b   Pleiades and Orion are constellations in the northern hemisphere.
c   "Dressed stone": stone that has been shaped and its faces have been smoothed.

30

¹³ Therefore
>the prudent one keeps quiet at a time like this, for it is an evil time.

>¹⁴ Seek good and not evil so that you may live,
>>and so the LORD God of Armies will be with you, just like you said.
>¹⁵ Hate evil,
>love good,
>establish justice in the gate;
>>perhaps the LORD God of Armies will be gracious to the remnant of Joseph.

¹⁶ Therefore the LORD God of Armies, my God, says this:
>"There will be wailing in every square;
>in every street they are saying, 'Woe! Woe!'
>They will call the *tenant* farmer to mourning and the professional mourners to weeping.
>¹⁷ There will be wailing in every vineyard, for I will pass through your midst," declares the LORD.

¹⁸ Woe to those who desire the day of the LORD! What is the day of the LORD to you? It'll be darkness, not light— ¹⁹ just like when a man flees before a lion and encounters a bear, or enters the house and rests his hand on the wall— and a snake bites him. ²⁰ Won't the day of the LORD be darkness and not light, thick darkness with no brightness in it?

²¹ *The Lord says,*
>"I hate and I reject your festivals;
>I cannot bear the stench of your solemn assemblies!*ᵃ*
>>²² If you should bring me burnt offerings and grain offerings, I won't accept them;
>>I won't look *with favor* upon your fellowship offerings of choice animals.
>>²³ Take the noise of your singing away from me.
>>I won't listen to the music from your harps.
>²⁴ Rather,
>>let justice roll on like waters and
>>righteousness like a never-failing stream.

²⁵ "Did you bring me sacrifices and grain offerings for forty years in the wilderness, O Israelites?
>²⁶ You lifted up Sikkuth your king and
>Kiyyun, your idols—*each* a star-god that you made for yourselves.*ᵇ*
>²⁷ Therefore
>>I will send you into exile beyond Damascus,"
>>>says the LORD, whose name is the God of Armies.

---

a   Literally, "I won't smell your assemblies."
b   "Sikkuth" and "Kiyyun" may refer to Assyrian gods. The Septuagint reads, "You have lifted up the shrine of your god Molech and the star of your god Rephan, your idols which you made for yourselves."

A Warning to the Complacent

¹ Woe to those who are complacent in Zion, and those who feel secure *worshiping* on Mount Samaria—

> you prominent citizens of the foremost of nations,
> *you* to whom the people of Israel[a] come.

² Go through Calneh and look.
Walk from there to Hamath, the great *city*.
Go down to Gath of the Philistines.

> Are they better than your *two* kingdoms?
> Is their territory larger than yours?

³ You *think you* are putting off the day of disaster, but you are bringing near a violent end.[b]

⁴ For you

> lie in beds decorated with ivory[c] and lounge on their couches,
>> eating lambs from the flock and calves from the midst of the stall,
> ⁵ improvise music on the harp and compose songs for yourselves like David, and
> ⁶ drink wine by the bowlful and anoint yourselves with the finest ointments—

yet you do not grieve over the ruin of Joseph.

⁷ Therefore

> now they will go at the head of the exiles.
> Their feasting and lounging will end.

⁸ The Lord God has sworn by himself.
This is a declaration of the Lord God of Armies:

> "I loathe Jacob's arrogance. I detest his citadels.
> I will deliver up this city and everything in it."
>> ⁹ If ten people should be left in one house, they'll die.
>>> ¹⁰ When his uncle, the one who anoints the body for burial,[d] lifts him up to carry out his bones from the house, he'll say to those in the innermost part of the house, "Is anyone left with you?" "No one," they'll reply. Then he'll say, "Hush! We must not mention the name of the Lord." ¹¹ For listen! The Lord has given the command: The great house will be smashed to pieces and the small house to bits.

> ¹² Do horses run on rocks?
> Does one plow *the sea* with oxen?
>> Yet you have turned justice into poison and the fruit of righteousness into bitterness.[e]

---

a   Literally, "the house of Israel."
b   Or "a seat of violence" or "a reign of violence." The Hebrew is ambiguous.
c   Literally, "beds of ivory."
d   The Hebrew for this word is uncertain.
e   Literally, "into wormwood," an herb with an extraordinarily bitter taste.

The Lord says,ᵃ

¹³ "You are rejoicing over nothing,

saying, 'Wasn't it by our own strength that we conquered the strong ones?'ᵇ

¹⁴ For look! I am raising up a nation over you, O house of Israel, declares the LORD God of Armies.

It will oppress you from Lebo Hamath to the valley of the Arabah."ᶜ

Amos 7

Three Visions

Locusts

¹ This is what the Lord GOD showed me. I saw it!

He was forming a swarm of locusts at the time when the spring crop starts to come upᵈ (I mean afterᵉ the harvest of the king's shareᶠ of the crops). ² When the locusts had finished devouring the vegetation on the land, I said, "Lord GOD, please forgive! How can Jacob stand? He is so small!"

³ The LORD relented concerning this, saying, "It will not come to pass."

Fire

⁴ This is what the Lord GOD showed me. I saw it!

The Lord GOD was calling for judgment by fire. It consumed the great deep and devoured the land. ⁵ I said, "Lord GOD, please stop! How can Jacob stand? He is so small!"

⁶ The Lord GOD relented concerning this, saying, "This will not happen either."

A Plumb Line

⁷ This is what he showed me. I saw it!

The Lord was standing with a plumb line in his hand on a wall that had been built true to plumb.ᵍ ⁸ The LORD said to me,

"What do you see, Amos?"

"A plumb line,"ʰ I replied.

The Lord said,

"Look! I am placing a plumb line in the middle of my people Israel. I'll spare them no longer.

⁹ The high-place shrines of Isaac will be made desolate, and
the sanctuaries of Israel will be ruined.
I'll rise up against the house of Jeroboam with a sword."

---

a   It is unclear whether the Lord begins speaking here or at the beginning of the previous or following verse.

b   Literally, "You are rejoicing in Lo Debar, saying, 'Didn't we take Karnaim for ourselves by our own strength?'" *Lo Debar* means "nothing," and *Karnaim* means "horns," which are symbols of strength.

c   I.e., the entire length of Israel's and Judah's territory.

d   Literally, "at the beginning of the spring crop."

e   Literally, "Look, that is after."

f   Literally, "the king's mowings."

g   Literally, "built on a wall of a plumb line." "Plumb line": a weighted line that is used to determine verticality.

h   The image contains a play on words. The Hebrew word for "plumb line," *anak*, sounds like the word for the first-person personal pronoun, *ani*. So Amos sees God as placing him as the plumb line.

Judgment on a False Prophet

[10] Amaziah, the priest at Bethel, sent word to Jeroboam king of Israel, saying, "Amos is forming a conspiracy against you in the midst of Israel. Your kingdom cannot endure all his actions.[a] [11] This is what Amos has said: 'Jeroboam will die by the sword, and Israel will certainly be removed from its land into exile.'"

[12] Amaziah said to Amos, "You *false* seer, go! Flee to Judah; eat food and prophesy there! [13] Don't prophesy anymore at Bethel, for it is the king's sanctuary and palace."

[14] Amos answered Amaziah: "I am neither a prophet nor the son of a prophet. I am a shepherd and a tender of sycamore fig trees. [15] But the LORD took me from following the flock and the LORD said to me, 'Go, prophesy to my people Israel.' [16] Now listen to the word of the LORD. You are saying, 'Don't prophesy against Israel nor speak against the house of Isaac.' [17] Therefore the LORD says this:

'Your wife will be a whore in the city, and
your sons and daughters will fall by the sword.
Your property will be measured and divided up,[b]
and you'll die in a foreign country.[c]
Israel will surely go into exile away from their land.'"

8 Amos

Your End Is Coming

[1] This is what the Lord GOD showed me: I saw it—a basket of summer fruit!

[2] He asked me, "What do you see, Amos?"

"A basket of *ripe* summer fruit,"[d] I answered.

Then the LORD said to me, "The end time has come for my people Israel. I'll spare them no longer. [3] The songs in the palace will turn into wailing on that day, declares the Lord GOD. There will be many corpses flung everywhere; it'll be silent."

[4] Listen to this, you who trample the needy and make an end of the humble in the land, [5] who ask,

"When will the New Moon *Festival* be over,
    so we can sell grain, and
the Sabbath *be ended,*
    so we can open the wheat *market,*
        reducing the measure and
        boosting the price,[e]
        cheating with dishonest scales,
    [6] buying the poor with silver and the needy for a pair of sandals,
        selling even the *inedible* refuse[f] with the wheat?"

---

a   Literally, "The land cannot bear all his words."
b   Literally, "will be divided by a *measuring* line."
c   Literally, "unclean country."
d   The image contains a play on words. The Hebrew word for "summer fruit," *qayits,* is close to the word for "end," *qets,* in the next sentence.
e   Literally, "reducing the ephah and boosting the shekel."
f   "*Inedible* refuse": dust, chaff, and other foreign matter that should have been removed from grain for sale.

⁷ The Lord has sworn by *himself, by* the Pride of Jacob, "I'll never forget any of their deeds.

⁸ "Doesn't the land tremble over all of this and everyone in it mourn?
For
    all of the land will rise up like the Nile;
      it'll be tossed around and subside like the Nile in Egypt.
⁹ "It will come about on that day, declares the Lord God,
    I'll make the sun go down at noon and darken the earth in broad daylight.
     ¹⁰ I'll turn your festivals into mourning and all your songs into laments.
    I'll cause you all to dress in sackcloth,^{*a*} and every head will be shaved.^{*b*}
    I'll make it like *a time of* mourning for an only son,
and the end will be like a bitter day.

¹¹ "Hear this! The days are coming, declares the Lord God, when
    I'll send famine on the land,
      not a famine of food nor thirst for water but from hearing messages from the Lord.
    ¹² People will stagger
      from sea to sea, from north to east, roaming about,
        seeking the Lord's message, but they won't find it.
¹³ "On that day
    beautiful virgins and young men will faint from thirst.
    ¹⁴ Those who swear by the idols^{*c*} of Samaria and say, 'As your god lives, O Dan,'
    or, 'As the god of^{*d*} Beersheba lives,' they will fall and not rise again."

Amos 9

Israel Will Be Destroyed and Restored

¹ I saw the Lord standing beside the altar, and he said,
    "Strike the tops of the pillars^{*e*} so that the thresholds shake. Bring them down on the heads of all *the people*, and the rest I'll slay with the sword! They won't have a fugitive who flees nor a refugee who escapes.
    ² If they dig as deep as Sheol,^{*f*}
      my hand will take them up from there.
    If they go up to the heavens,
      I'll bring them down from there.
    ³ If they hide on the summit of Mount Carmel,
      I'll hunt them down and take them from there.
    If they hide from my eyes at the bottom of the sea,
      I'll command the serpent, and it will bite them.

---

a Literally, "I'll make sackcloth come upon all your loins."
b A shaved head and wearing sackcloth were signs of mourning.
c Literally, "by the guilt."
d From the Septuagint; Masoretic text: "the way of."
e Literally, "the capitals," the decorative elements on top of pillars.
f Literally, "dig into Sheol."

⁴ If they go into captivity before their enemies,
   I'll command the sword to slay them there.
I will set my eyes against them for disaster and not for prosperity."

⁵ The Lord GOD of Armies is the one who touches the earth and it melts, and everyone in it mourns. *At his command* all of it rises and subsides like the Nile of Egypt; ⁶ it is he who built his upper chamber in the heavens and sank its foundation^a in the earth, who calls for the waters in the sea and pours them out on the face of the earth: The LORD is his name.

⁷ The LORD declares,
   "Aren't you like the Cushites to me, O Israelites?
Didn't I bring the Israelites up from Egypt, the Philistines from Caphtor,^b and the Arameans from Kir?^c
⁸ See! The eyes of the LORD are on the sinful kingdom.
   I'll destroy it from the face of the earth.
   Yet I won't totally destroy the family of Jacob," declares the LORD.
   ⁹ "Watch out! I will give the command, and
   I'll shake the people of Israel among all the nations
      like *one* sifts in a sieve, but not the smallest pebble^d will fall to the ground.
      ¹⁰ All the sinners among my people, those who claim, 'The disaster won't overtake or confront us,' will die by the sword.
¹¹ On that day
   I will raise up David's fallen tent;
   I will shore up its breaches and raise up its ruins;
   I will rebuild it like in former days
      ¹² so that they may possess the remnant of Edom and all the nations that are called by my name, declares the LORD, who will do this.

¹³ "Listen! The days are coming, declares the LORD, when
   the plowman will overtake the reaper,
   the one who treads grapes will overtake the one who casts seed, and
   the mountains will drip with grape juice—the heights will flow *with it.*
¹⁴ I will bring back the captives of my people Israel.
   They'll rebuild desolate cities and live *in them.*
   They'll plant vineyards and drink their wine.
   They'll tend gardens and eat their fruit.
¹⁵ I will plant them in their land, and they'll never again be uprooted from the land I have given to them, says the LORD your God."

---

a   Literally, "founded his vaulted dome." A reference to the space ancients thought was above the earth and sky and below whatever was above that (clouds, waters, etc.). Some thought of it as an architectural vault, a support like an upside down bowl, though its solidity is uncertain). See Genesis 1:6.

b   "Caphtor": While not certain, many identify Caphtor with f Crete, about 600 miles west of Lebanon.

c   "Kir" (i.e., Enclosure) may be a reference to several places, including, perhaps, Kir Hareseth

d   Literally, "not a pebble."

Obadiah

Obadiah's Vision[a]

¹ This is what the Lord GOD says to Edom:
    "We have heard a report[b] from the LORD,
      and an ambassador was sent among the nations *to say*,
        'Rise, let us rise against *Edom* for battle.'"

Edom's Pride

² "Look! I will make you insignificant among the nations; you'll be extremely despised. ³ The arrogance of your heart has fooled you. *You* sit in the heights, inhabiting the cracks in the cliffside, saying in *your* heart, 'Who could bring me down to the ground?'

Edom's Destruction

⁴ "Even if you fly as high as the eagle and establish your nest among the stars, from there I'll bring you down, declares the LORD. ⁵ If thieves came to you—robbers at night—oh, how you'll be destroyed! Wouldn't they steal only as much as they could carry?[c] If grape pickers came to you, wouldn't they leave a few grapes?[d] ⁶ O, how Esau will be ransacked, his hidden treasures searched for *and found*! ⁷ All your allies[e] will drive you to the border; your friends[f] will fool you and conquer you. *Those who eat* your bread will set a trap for you. No one will be aware of it."[g]

⁸ The LORD declares, "In that day, will I not destroy the wise men from Edom and understanding from *everyone on* the mountain of Esau? ⁹ O Teman! Your warriors will be shattered so that everyone from the mountain of Esau will be cut down by slaughter. ¹⁰ You'll be covered with shame and destroyed forever because of violence against your brother Jacob. ¹¹ On the day you stood aloof, on the day strangers carried off his wealth and foreigners entered his gates and cast lots for Jerusalem, you too were like one of them.

¹² "But you must not gloat in[h] your brother *Israel's* day, the day of his calamity.
    Don't rejoice over the children of Judah in the day of their destruction.
    Don't boast in the day of *their* distress.
      ¹³ In the day of their disaster,
        don't enter the gate of my people. In the day of their disaster,
        don't even look on their misery. In the day of their disaster,
        don't grab their wealth.

---

a   This heading is part of the Hebrew text.
b   Literally, "a heard thing."
c   Literally, "steal *until they had* enough?"
d   Literally, "some gleanings"; that is, produce left behind after harvesting or threshing.
e   Literally, "All the men of your covenant."
f   Literally, "men of your peace."
g   Or "They have no understanding."
h   Literally, "not look upon."

¹⁴ In the day of their distress,

> don't stand at the crossroads to cut off their refugees. In the day of their distress
>
> don't hand over their survivors *to anyone.*

¹⁵ For the day of the Lord is near and upon all nations.

> As you have done, it will be done to you.
>
> Your deeds will return on your own head.
>
>> ¹⁶ For as you drank on my holy mountain, so all the nations will drink continually;
>>
>>> they'll drink and swallow and disappear.ᵃ

¹⁷ "But on Mount Zion there will be deliverance.

> It will be holy, and the family of Jacob will possess their inheritance.
>
>> ¹⁸ The family of Jacob will be a fire, and the family of Joseph will be a flame,
>>
>> but the family of Esau will be stubble.
>>
>>> They'll set them on fire and consume them.
>>>
>>> There'll be no survivors for the family of Esau."

For the Lord has spoken.

Possessors of the Land

¹⁹ *The people from* the south

> will possess the mountain of Esau, and

the people from the lowlands

> will possess *the land of* the Philistines and the fields of Ephraim and Samaria.

Benjamin

> *will possess* Gilead.

²⁰ These exiles from the army of the children of Israel

> *will possess the land* of the Canaanites as far *north* as Zarephath.

The exiles from Jerusalem (the ones who are in Sepharadᵇ)

> will possess the cities of the south.

²¹ The deliverers will go up to Mount Zion to governᶜ the mountains of Esau, and the kingdom will be the Lord's.

---

a Literally, "and be as nonexistent."

b Sepharad's location is unknown.

c Literally, "to judge."

Jonah

Jonah Is Called to Go to Nineveh

¹ The word of the LORD came to Jonah son of Amittai:
² "Arise and go to Nineveh, the great city.
Announce to it that their wickedness has come up before me."

Jonah Runs from God

³ *However,* Jonah fled from the presence of the LORD to Tarshish. He went down to Joppa and found a ship going there. He paid the fare and boarded to go with them to Tarshish, away from the presence of the LORD. ⁴ The LORD hurled a great wind on the sea. It was a huge ocean storm, and the ship was close to breaking apart.ᵃ ⁵ The sailors were afraid, and each one cried out to his own god. They began to throw the ship's cargo into the sea to lighten it for them. But Jonah had gone down to the lower deck, lain down, and fallen deeply asleep. ⁶ The captain came to him and said, "How can you sleep? Get up and call on your god! Perhaps he will be concerned for us, and we won't perish."

⁷ Each one was saying to his neighbor, "Come, let's cast lots to find out on whose account this disaster *has come* upon us." They cast lots, and the lot fell on Jonah. ⁸ They said to him, "Tell us, on whose account has this disaster come upon us? What is your occupation, and where have you come from? What is your country, and from what people do you come?"

⁹ He replied, "I am a Hebrew. I fear the LORD, the God of heaven, who made the sea and the dry land."

¹⁰ Then the men were terribly afraid and said to him, "What is this you have done?" For the men knew that he was fleeing from the presence of the LORD, because he had told them so. ¹¹ They asked him, "What should we do with you so the sea will calm down for us?" (The sea was continuing to rage.ᵇ)

¹² He replied, "Lift me up and hurl me into the sea, and it will quiet down for you. For I know that this gale has come upon you because of me."

¹³ But instead, the men rowed hard to return to shore, but they could not *get there* because the sea continued to rage against them. ¹⁴ They called upon the LORD and said, "Please, O LORD! Do not let us perish on account of this man's life. May you not hold us accountable for innocent blood, for you, LORD, have done just as you desired." ¹⁵ Then they lifted Jonah up and hurled him into the sea, and the sea stopped its raging. ¹⁶ Then the men were terrified of the LORD and offered a sacrifice to him and took vows. ¹⁷ The LORD appointed a huge fish to swallow Jonah, and he was in the fish's belly for three days and three nights.

---

a   Literally, "and the ship was reckoned to be broken apart."
b   Literally, "was continuing to storm" Also in verse 13.

2 Jonah

Jonah Prays

¹ Jonah prayed to the Lᴏʀᴅ his God from the belly of the fish ² and said,
"I called to the Lᴏʀᴅ out of my distress,
  and he answered me;
I cried for help from the darkness*ᵃ* of the grave,
  and you listened to my voice.

³ "You had thrown me into the depths, the heart of the seas.
  The currents surrounded me; all your breakers and waves passed
  over me.
⁴ As for me, I said,
  'I have been driven from your sight;
  nevertheless, I will again look toward your holy temple.'

⁵ "Waters engulfed me,*ᵇ* and I almost died;
  the deep surrounded me; seaweed bound my head.
⁶ I descended to the foundations of the mountains;
  the earth hemmed me in*ᶜ* forever.
But you, O Lᴏʀᴅ my God, have brought up my life from the pit.
⁷ When my life was ebbing away, I remembered the Lᴏʀᴅ.
My prayer came to you, to your holy temple.

⁸ "Those who revere worthless idols forsake *the Lord's* lovingkindness.
⁹ But as for me,
  I will sacrifice to you with a voice of thanksgiving.
  What I have vowed, I will pay,
    for salvation is from the Lᴏʀᴅ."

¹⁰ Then the Lᴏʀᴅ spoke to the fish, and it vomited Jonah onto dry land.

3 Jonah

Jonah Preaches in Nineveh

¹ The word of the Lᴏʀᴅ came to Jonah a second time:
  ² "Arise and go to Nineveh, the great city. Proclaim to it the message that I will
  speak to you."
³ So Jonah got up and went to Nineveh, according to the word of the Lᴏʀᴅ. Now
Nineveh was a great big city—*it took* three days to walk *through it.* ⁴ Jonah proceeded
to enter the city, and on the first day he walked around proclaiming, "In forty days
Nineveh will be overthrown!"

---

a Literally, "the belly."
b Literally, "Waters encompassed up to my soul."
c Literally, "the earth's bars around me."

Nineveh Repents and God Relents

[5] The people of Nineveh believed God. They proclaimed a fast and put on sackcloth, from the greatest to the least of them. [6] When news reached the king of Nineveh, he got up from his throne, took off his royal robe, put on sackcloth, and sat down in ashes. [7a] He issued this proclamation in Nineveh:

Call to Fasting and Repentance

[7c] Neither people nor livestock, herds nor flocks, may taste anything at all.
Do not feed them nor water them.
[8] Let *all* people and livestock wear sackcloth.
Let them call to God urgently.
Let each person repent of their evil ways and from the violence that is in their hands.
[9] Perhaps God will turn and relent—turn away from his fierce anger, so we will not perish!

[7b] *By Order of*
The King and His Nobles

[10] When God saw what they did, that they had repented from their evil ways, he relented from the disaster that he had threatened to do to them and did not do it.

Jonah 4

God Rebukes Jonah's Self-Pity

[1] This was terrible in Jonah's opinion,[a] and he was angry. [2] He prayed to the LORD and said, "Now, LORD, didn't I say this when I was in my own country? This is what I tried to prevent by fleeing to Tarshish![b] For I know that you are a gracious and merciful God, slow to anger and abounding in loyal love, relenting from calamity. [3] Now, O LORD, take my life from me, for it is better for me to die than live!"

[4] The LORD said, "Do you have a good reason to be angry?"

[5] Jonah went out of the city and sat down to the east of it. He made a shelter for himself and sat beneath it in the shade, until he could see what would happen to the city. [6] So the LORD God appointed a plant to come up over Jonah and shade his head and deliver him from his discomfort. Jonah was thrilled about the plant. [7] But the next day at dawn, God assigned a worm, and it attacked the plant, and it withered. [8] When the sun came up, God arranged for a hot east wind. *In addition*, the sun beat down on Jonah's head such that he became faint and begged to die,[c] saying, "It would be better for me to die than live."

---

a Literally, "This was a great evil in Jonah's eyes."
b Or "This is why I fled to Tarshish previously."
c Literally, "He asked his soul to die."

⁹Then God said to him, "Is there a good reason for you to be angry about the plant?"

And Jonah said to God, "There is a good reason—*enough* for me to be angry enough to *wish I were* dead!"

¹⁰The Lord said, "You had pity on the plant, which you did not tend, nor did you make it grow. It came up overnight and died overnight.*ᵃ* ¹¹As for me, should I not have pity on Nineveh, the great city, in which there are more than 120,000 human beings who do not know their right hand from their left,*ᵇ* as well as many livestock?"

---

a Literally, "which is a son of night and a son of night perished."

b This means that either (1) more than 120,000 inhabitants of Nineveh, being Gentiles, did not know God's moral requirements, so they did not know right from wrong; or (2) more than 120,000 children in the city could not be expected to know God's moral requirements because of their age. Both options point out that God never wants to punish the ignorant.

Micah

Part I. The Lord's Judgment

¹ The word of the Lᴏʀᴅ that came to Micah of *the town of* Moresheth
    in the days of Jotham, Ahaz, and Hezekiah, kings of Judah,ᵃ
    which he saw regarding Samaria and Jerusalem.

Judgment upon Samaria and Jerusalem

² Listen, all peoples! Pay attention, earth and everything in it!
    The Lord Gᴏᴅ has become a witness against you, the Lord from his holy temple.
³ For watch!
    The Lᴏʀᴅ is coming out from his place.
    He is coming down and treading on the high places of the land.
  ⁴ The mountains melt beneath him;
    the valleys split apart
      like wax before the fire,
      like water rushing downhill.

⁵ All of this *is happening* because of
    Jacob's transgression and
    the sins of the family of Israel.
      What is Jacob's transgression? Isn't it *the calf-idols at* Samaria?
      What are these high-place shrines in Judah? Shouldn't worshipᵇ be *only*
      in Jerusalem?

⁶ *The Lord declares,*
    "I will make Samaria a heap of ruins in the open country, places to plant a vineyard.
    I will pour her stones into the valley and expose her foundations.
  ⁷ All her idols will be smashed,
      and all her *sacred* prostitutes' wages will be burned in the fire.
    I will make all her images a desolate *pile.*
      For she gathered them from the wages of a prostitute, and to the wages
      of a prostitute they will return."

⁸ For this reason I, *Micah,* will
    weep and wail,
    go about barefoot and naked, and
    howl like the jackals and mourn like an owl.
⁹ For Samaria's illnessᶜ is incurable;
    it has come up to Judah and even reached the gate of my people,
    even to Jerusalem.

---

a Jotham reigned from 750 to 735 BC; Ahaz from 735 to 716 BC; and Hezekiah from 716 to 687 BC.
b Literally, "Shouldn't it be?"
c Literally, "blow" or "wound."

¹⁰ Do not report it *to our enemies* in Gath;
   do not weep at all *before them.*
Instead,
      roll in the dust at Beth Ophrah (*i.e.,* House of Dust).
   ¹¹ Pass by naked and ashamed, you who live in Shaphir (*i.e.,* Pleasantness).
         Those who live in Zaanan*ᵃ* won't come out.
         Beth Ezel (*i.e.,* House of Removal) is in mourning,
            for he has removed your support from you.
         ¹² Those living in Maroth (*i.e.,* Bitterness) have become weak, *waiting* for relief,*ᵇ*
            for disaster has come down from the Lord to the gate of Jerusalem.

¹³ Hitch the chariot to the horses, you who live in Lachish
         (she is where the sin of Daughter Zion began),
      for the transgressions of Israel have been found in you.
¹⁴ Therefore
      you will give parting gifts to Moresheth Gath.
      The town of Aczib (*i.e.,* Deception*ᶜ*) will be a deception to the kings of Israel.
¹⁵ What is more:
      A conqueror is coming to you, inhabitants of Mareshah, and
      the nobles*ᵈ* of Israel will flee to Adullam.*ᵉ*

¹⁶ So
      shave yourself and be bald*ᶠ* because of the *loss of the* children in whom you delight.
      Make your baldness even more complete,*ᵍ* like the *head of an* eagle,
         for they will go away from you into exile.

2 *Micah*

Judgment upon Oppressors

¹ Woe to those who consider iniquity and plan evil on their beds!
         At morning light they do it, for it is in the power of their hands.
      ² They covet fields and seize them, and houses and take them.
         They oppress a person and their family, a person and their inheritance.

³ Therefore the Lord says this: "Listen!
         I am planning disaster for this clan, from which you cannot save yourselves.*ʰ*
         You won't walk proudly, for it will be a time of disaster.
      ⁴ In that day they will taunt you and lament bitterly, *but insincerely,* saying
         'We are utterly destroyed! My people's portion is changed!
         How he removes it from me! He has divided up our fields for traitors!'

---

a   "Zaanan" is a pun on the word for "come out."
b   Literally, "for good."
c   Literally, "the houses of Aczib."
d   Literally, "the glory."
e   Literally, "will enter." Adullam was a Canaanite city.
f   "Be bald": a shaved head was a sign of mourning.
g   Literally, "even larger."
h   Literally, "from which you cannot remove your necks."

⁵ Therefore you will have no one to determine the boundaries*ᵃ* for you when lots are cast*ᵇ to divide the land* in the assembly of the Lord.

⁶ "'Do not preach,' *they say.* 'Do not preach about these things.
  No reprimands will move us back.'
⁷ Does anyone ask,*ᶜ* family of Jacob,
    'Is the Spirit of the Lord impatient?
    Are these his deeds?'
  Don't my words do good for the one who walks uprightly?
⁸ My people have risen up as an enemy recently.
    You strip the rich robe off of unsuspecting passersby, like those who return from war.*ᵈ*
      ⁹ You are driving the women of my people from their pleasant homes.
      You take away my splendor from their children forever.

¹⁰ "Get up and go,
    for this is not the place to rest,
    because of the uncleanness that brings on destruction, painful destruction.
      ¹¹ If someone spoke lies through a deceiving spirit, *declaring,* 'I will prophesy wine and beer for you,' that would be just the prophet for this people.

¹² "I will surely gather all of you, Jacob;
  I will surely assemble the remnant of Israel.
  I will place them together like sheep in an enclosure,
    like sheep in the middle of their pasture. It will be *loud* with the noise of *many* people. ¹³ The one who breaks through will lead them. They will break through and pass out of the gate; they will go out of it. Their king will pass before them, the Lord at their head."

Micah 3

Judgment upon Israel's Leaders

¹ I said,
    "Listen, heads of Jacob and chiefs of the family of Israel.
      Shouldn't you understand justice?
      ² *You are* haters of good and lovers of evil.
        You flay the skin from *the poor* and the meat from their bones.
          ³ You eat the flesh of my people.
            You strip off their skin, break their bones, and chop them up*ᵉ* like *meat* for the pot, like flesh for the cauldron."

⁴ Then they will cry out to the Lord, but he won't answer them.
  He will hide his face from them at that time, because they made their deeds evil.

---

a Literally, "to stretch a measuring line."
b Literally, "when by lot."
c Literally, "Is it asked."
d I.e., like victorious soldiers who are plundering civilians.
e Literally, "and spread them out."

⁵ The Lᴏʀᴅ says this about the prophets who are leading my people astray:
"They proclaim, 'Peace!' when they have *something* to eat,[a]
but they declare holy war on those who refuse to feed them[b].
⁶ Therefore
at night you will have no visions;
you will have no divination in the darkness.
The sun will set on the prophets, and the day will be dark for them.
⁷ The seers will be ashamed, and the diviners will be embarrassed.
They will all cover their faces[c] because there is no answer from God."

⁸ But as for me, I am filled
with power and the Spirit of the Lᴏʀᴅ,
with justice and might,
to declare to Jacob his transgression and to Israel his sin.

⁹ Listen to this, heads of the family of Jacob and chiefs of the house of Israel, you who
abhor justice and twist everything that is right, and
¹⁰ build Zion with bloodshed and Jerusalem with injustice.
¹¹ Her leaders dispense justice for bribes, and her priests teach for a price.
Her prophets practice divination for silver,
yet they lean on the Lᴏʀᴅ, saying,
"Isn't the Lᴏʀᴅ among us? Disaster won't come upon us."
¹² Therefore because of you,
Zion will be a plowed field, and
Jerusalem will be a heap of ruins.
The temple mount will be a mound overgrown by thickets.

Part 2. The Lord Reigns

4 *Micah*

The Lord's Reign in the Last Days

¹ It will be in last days
that the mountain of the Lᴏʀᴅ's temple will be established at the head of the mountains.
It will be lifted up higher than the heights.
The peoples will stream to it.
² Many nations will come and say,
"Come, let's go up to the mountain of the Lᴏʀᴅ,
to the temple of the God of Jacob.
He will teach us his ways, and we will walk in his paths."
For instruction will go out from Zion and the word of the Lᴏʀᴅ from Jerusalem.

---

a   Literally, "when they chew with their teeth."
b   Literally, "who put nothing in their mouths."
c   Literally, "all grasp the mustache."

³ The Lord will judge between many peoples and render decisions for strong nations far away.

> They will beat their swords into plowshares and their spears into pruning hooks.
> Nation will not take up sword against nation, nor will they train for war anymore.
> ⁴ Everyone will sit under their own vine and fig tree, with no one to make them afraid,
>> for the mouth of the Lord of Armies has spoken.
> ⁵ Though all the peoples may walk, each in the name of their god, as for us, we will walk in the name of the Lord our God forever and ever.

⁶ The Lord declares,
> "On that day,
>> I will gather up the lame and assemble those who were driven away,
>>> even those I have afflicted.
>> ⁷ I will make the lame a remnant, and those driven away a powerful nation.
>> The Lord will reign over them on Mount Zion, from now to forever.
> ⁸ As for you, watchtower of the flock, hill of Daughter Zion,
>> to you it will come; the former dominion will be restored.ᵃ
>> Kingship *will return* to Daughter Jerusalem."ᵇ

⁹ Now why do you cry out?
> Is there no king in you?
> Or has your counselor perished *so* that agony has gripped you like a woman in labor?

¹⁰ Writhe and burst forth, Daughter Zion, like a woman in labor,
> for now you are going out from the city.
> You will live in the open country and go on to Babylon.
>> There you will be rescued.
>> The Lord will redeem you there from the hand of your enemies.

¹¹ Now many nations are gathered against you, saying, "Let her be defiled, so our eyes may gaze atᶜ Zion's *shame*."

¹² But
> they do not know the plans of the Lord;
> they do not understand his purpose,
>> for he has gathered them like sheaves to the threshing floor.

¹³ Arise and thresh,ᵈ Daughter Zion,
> for I will make your horn iron and your hooves bronze.
> You will crush many peoples.
> You will devote their unjust gain to the Lord and their wealth to the Lord of all the earth.

---

a Literally, "will come."
b The quote may continue through verse 13.
c Or "gloat over."
d "Thresh": to separate a plant's grain from the stalk, usually by flailing or using a revolving device.

5 Micah

The Lord Will Rescue Israel

¹ Now form regiments, city of troops,ᵃ
  for they have laid siege against us.
  They will strike the ruler of Israel on the cheek with a rod.

² *The Lord says,*
  "But as for you, Bethlehem *of* Ephrathah, *though* you are small among the
  clans of Judah,
    one who will be the ruler of Israel for me will come out of you.
      His originsᵇ are from long ago, from ancient times.
        ³ Therefore he will give them up *to wandering* until the time when she
        who is in labor has given birth, and the rest of his brothers return to
        the Israelites.
      ⁴ He will stand and shepherd his flock
        in the power of the Lᴏʀᴅ,
        in the majestic name of the Lᴏʀᴅ his God.
          And they will live securely,ᶜ for
        he will be great at that time, to the ends of the earth.
        ⁵ He will be *the source of* peace."

  When the Assyrians invade our land,
  when they tread upon our citadels,
    we will raise against them seven shepherds, even eight leaders of troops.
      ⁶ They will rule
        Assyria with the sword,
        the land of Nimrod at its entrances.
  The Lᴏʀᴅᵈ will rescue us from the Assyrians when they enter our land, when
  they trample our borders.

⁷ The remnant of Jacob will be in the midst of many peoples,
  like dew from the Lᴏʀᴅ,
  like showers on vegetation,
    showers that do not wait for anyone or delay for mortals.ᵉ
⁸ The remnant of Jacob will be
  among the nations,
  in the midst of many peoples,
  like a lion among the animals of the forest,
  like a young lion among flocks of sheep, which tramples and tears as it passes
  through, and there is no one to rescue them.
⁹ You will lift up your hand over your enemies, and all your foes will be cut off.

---

a Literally, "daughter of troops."
b Literally, "His goings out."
c Literally, "they will remain."
d Literally, "He."
e Literally, "for the sons of man."

¹⁰ The Lord declares,
"It will be on that day that
I will

remove^a your horses from among you and destroy your chariots;
¹¹ remove the cities of your land and throw down all your fortifications;
¹² remove sorceries from your hand,
and you will no longer have mediums among you;
¹³ remove your carved images and sacred stones from your midst,
and you will no longer bow down to what your hands have made;
¹⁴ uproot your Asherim^b from among you, and
level your cities."
¹⁵ I will take vengeance in anger and wrath on those nations that have not obeyed."

Part 3. The Lord's Justice and Mercy

Micah 6

God's Case Against Israel

¹ Listen to what the Lord says:
"Stand up and argue your case before the mountains;
let the hills hear your voice.
² Listen, O mountains, to the Lord's indictment;
listen, you everlasting foundations of the earth,
for the Lord is going to court against his people,^{c}
and he is arguing it out with Israel, *saying*,
³ "My people, what have I done to you?
How have I burdened you? Answer me!
⁴ For I brought you up from Egypt;
I redeemed you from the house of slavery.
I sent Moses, Aaron, and Miriam before you.
⁵ "My people!
Remember what Balak king of Moab advised and
remember how Balaam son of Beor answered him.
Remember your journey from Shittim to Gilgal^d
so that you may know the Lord's righteous acts."

---

a   Literally, "I will cut off." And verses 11–13.
b   "Asherim": idols related to Asherah, the Canaanite goddess of the sea.
c   Literally, "for a lawsuit belongs to the Lord with his people."
d   The Israelites engaged in immorality at Shittim (see Numbers 25), yet God took them to Gilgal, their first
camp in the promised land.

⁶ With what can I come before the Lord and bow down before the God on high?
  Should I come before him with burnt offerings, with year-old calves?
    ⁷ Will the Lord be pleased with thousands of rams or myriad*ᵃ* rivers of oil?
  Shall I give my firstborn for my transgression,
    the fruit of my body for the sin of my soul?
⁸ He has told you, O mortal, what is good.
  What does the Lord require from you? But
    to act justly,
    to love mercy,*ᵇ* and
    to walk humbly with your God.

⁹ The voice of the Lord calls out to the city—and to fear your name is wise—
  "Pay attention to the rod *of punishment;*
    think of who has assigned its job.*ᶜ*
  ¹⁰ Shall I still forget
    the treasures *gained through* wickedness in the house of the wicked,*ᵈ*
    and the short measure,*ᵉ* which is accursed?
      ¹¹ Should I declare as innocent the wicked scales and the bag full of
      fraudulent weights?

God's Punishment of Israel

¹² "Your rich people are full of violence.
  Its inhabitants speak falsely, and the tongues in their mouths are deceitful.
    ¹³ So also I have begun to strike you, destroying you because of your sin.
      ¹⁴ You will eat but not be satisfied.
      I will put darkness in your midst.*ᶠ*
      You will save up but not accumulate *much,*
        and whatever you accumulate I will give to the sword.
      ¹⁵ You will sow but not reap.
      You will tread olives but not anoint yourselves with oil.
      You will tread grapes but not drink the wine.
¹⁶ "You have
    kept the statutes of *King* Omri*ᵍ* and *done* all the evil deeds of the family of
    Ahab—walked in their counsels.
      So I will give you over to destruction and your inhabitants to horror.
      You will bear my people's disgrace."

---

a Literally, "with tens of thousands."
b Or "to love lovingkindness" or "to love loyal love."
c Literally, "for who has appointed it."
d Or "Are there still wicked treasures in the house of the wicked?" or "Is there still a person in the wicked house and treasures of wickedness?" The Hebrew is uncertain.
e "Short measure": one less than the correct amount.
f From one edition of the Septuagint; Masoretic text: "Your dung will be in your midst."
g Omri was an especially wicked king who ruled over the northern kingdom of Israel in the 800s BC. See 1 Kings 16:16–28.

Israel's Problems and Faith

¹ *Israel says,*

"Woe is me!

For I have become like one who gathers summer fruit. like grape pickers.

There is no bunch of grapes *for me* to eat or any of the early figs I crave.

² Faithful people have perished from the earth.

There is not one person who is upright.

All that remain[a] lie in wait to shed blood.

Each one hunts the other with a net.

³ Their hands are skilled at doing evil.

The prince demands *favors*;

the judge *renders decisions* for a bribe, and

the powerful dictate their evil desires.

They all conspire[b] together.

⁴ The best of them is like a briar;

the most upright is *worse than* a thorn hedge.

On the day *you post* your watchmen, your punishment *from God* will come.

Now is the time for their confusion."

⁵ *The Lord says,*

"Do not trust in a neighbor.

Do not rely on a friend.

Guard your lips[c] from the woman who lies in your embrace.[d]

⁶ For

a son disdains a father;

a daughter rises up against her mother;

a daughter-in-law despises her mother-in-law; and

a person's enemies are the members of their own household."

⁷ *Micah responds,*

"As for me,

I will watch expectantly for the LORD;

I will wait for God, my Savior.

My God will hear me.

⁸ Do not rejoice over me, my enemy.

Though I have fallen, I will rise;

though I sit in darkness, the LORD is my light.

⁹ "Because I have sinned against him, I will bear the LORD's wrath until he pleads my case and works justice for me.

---

a   Literally, "All of them."
b   Literally, "They weave it."
c   Literally, "Guard the opening of your mouth."
d   Literally, "in your bosom."

He will bring me into the light, and I will see his righteousness. ¹⁰ My enemy, she who says to me, "Where is the Lᴏʀᴅ your God?" will see and be covered with shame. My eyes will look on her, and at that time she will be trampled on like mud in the streets."

God Will Rescue Israel

¹¹ *Jerusalem, there will be* a day for building your walls.
　Israel, on that day your boundary will be extended.
　　¹² They will come to *honor* you
　　from
　　　　Assyria and
　　　　the cities of Egypt, from
　　　　Egypt to the Euphrates River, from
　　　　sea to sea and
　　　　mountain to mountain.
¹³ The earth will be a desolation
　　because of its inhabitants and the results of their deeds.

¹⁴ *O Lord*,
　　shepherd your people with your rod.
　　　　They are the sheep of your inheritance living in isolation in the forest, in the midst of a fruitful pasture.ᵃ
　　Let them feed in Bashan and Gilead,ᵇ like in days long ago.

¹⁵ *The Lord says*,
　　"Like in the days when you came out from Egypt,
　　I will show you wonders."
　　¹⁶ The nations will see and be ashamed of all their *imagined* power.
　　　　They will put their hands over their mouths, and their ears will become deaf.
　　　　¹⁷ They will lick dust like a serpent, like snakes that slither on the earth.
　　　　They will come
　　　　　　trembling out of their densᶜ to the Lᴏʀᴅ our God,
　　　　　　full of fear, standing in awe because of you.

¹⁸ Who is like you, God,
　　who takes away iniquity and passes over transgression for the remnant of his inheritance?

He does not hold onto his anger forever,
　　for he delights in loyal love.
　　¹⁹ He will again be merciful to us.
He will tread our iniquities underfoot.
　　Lord, you will throw all our sins into the depths of the sea.
　　　²⁰ You will give truth to Jacob and loyal love to Abraham,
　　　　like you swore to our ancestors in earlier days.

---

a Literally, "Carmel," referring to the rich lands around Mount Carmel.
b "Bashan and Gilead": two lush areas.
c Literally, "out of their strongholds."

Nahum

¹ The book of the vision of Nahum the Elkoshite.*ª* The message concerning Nineveh.

The Awesomeness of God

² The Lord
    is a jealous God who wreaks vengeance—
        wreaks vengeance and is full of wrath,
        wreaks vengeance on his foes and reserves wrath for his enemies.
³ The Lord is slow to anger and great in power.
    the Lord certainly does not acquit *the wicked.*
  His way is in the windstorm and the rainstorm;
    the clouds are the dust of his feet.
⁴ He rebukes the sea and dries it up;
  he makes all the rivers run dry.
    Bashan and Carmel wither; the blossoms of Lebanon wither.
⁵ The mountains quake because of him, and the hills melt away;
    the earth buckles and heaves*ᵇ* at his presence—the world and all who live in it.

⁶ Who can stand before his wrath?
  Who can endure his burning anger?
    His indignation is poured out like fire,
    and boulders are shattered before him.

⁷ The Lord is good, a fortress in a time of distress;
    he knows those who take refuge in him.
⁸ But with an overwhelming flood he will make an end of Nineveh;*ᶜ*
    he will pursue his enemies into darkness.

A Warning to Nineveh

⁹ What plans will you make against the Lord?
    He will make a total shambles of it.
    His distress *upon you* won't *need to* rise up twice.
        ¹⁰ For his enemies*ᵈ* are like tangled thorns or drunkards as they drink.
            They will be consumed like stubble that is fully dry.
        ¹¹ Yet a wicked counselor, one who plots evil against the Lord, has gone out
            from you.

---

a The location of Elkosh is uncertain.
b Literally, "the earth lifts up."
c Literally, "its place."
d Literally, "For they."

Nineveh Will Be Defeated

¹² The Lᴏʀᴅ says this *to Israel*:

"Though *Assyria is* at full strength and *has* numerous *allies*, they will be cut off and pass away;

I have afflicted you, but I will afflict you no longer.

¹³ But now I will break Assyria's yoke[a] from upon you and tear off your shackles."

¹⁴ The Lᴏʀᴅ has commanded concerning you, *Assyria*:[b]

"Your name won't be perpetuated any longer.

I will eliminate the carved idols and the molten metal images of the temple of your gods.

I will prepare your grave,

for you are despicable."

¹⁵ Notice! There on the mountains—the feet of one who brings good news, who announces peace!

Celebrate your feasts, Judah; fulfill your vows,

for the wicked won't invade you anymore.

All of them will be destroyed.

2 Nahum

¹ An attacker[c] has gone up against you.

Guard the rampart;

watch the road;

brace yourselves;[d]

marshal all your strength.

² For the Lᴏʀᴅ has returned the splendor of Jacob like the splendor of Israel,

though marauders laid waste to them and their grapevines are ruined.

³ His warriors' shields are red; his men of war are dressed in scarlet.

The steel on the chariots flashes like fire on the day he has set *to march*;

they brandish *spears* of juniper.

⁴ The chariots race around in the streets;

they rush back and forth in the squares;

their appearance is like torches; they dash here and there like lightning.

⁵ Nineveh remembers his nobles;

they stumble on the march;

they hurry to her wall, and the protective shield is secured.

⁶ The gates of the rivers are opened; the palace collapses.[e]

---

a Literally, "his yoke."
b Or Nineveh, the capital of the Assyrian Empire and largest city in the world at that time.
c Literally, "One who scatters."
d Literally, "gird up your loins."
e Literally, "is melted."

Its Treasures Will Be Carried Away

⁷ It is established: Nineveh is exiled and carried away.
  The lamenting of her handmaidens sounds like doves;
  they beat their breasts.
⁸ Nineveh was like a pool of water throughout her days,
  but now her people are fleeing.
  Its nobles cry,
    "Stop! Stop!" But no one turns back.
  ⁹ *Its enemies cry,*
    "Plunder the silver! Plunder the gold!"
    There is no end to the supply, to the wealth of all its treasures.ᵃ
  ¹⁰ She is empty, desolate, devastated!
    Hearts have melted and knees are knocking!
    Her body is trembling,ᵇ and every face grows pale.

The City Will Be Destroyed

¹¹ Where *now* is the lions' den,
    the feeding place of young lions,
    where the lion, lioness, and cubs prowled with nothing to fear?
  ¹² The lion tore enough *prey* for his cubs;
  he strangled *enough* for his lioness,
    filled his lair with prey and his den with the kill.

¹³ The Lᴏʀᴅ of Armies declares,
    "See! I am against you!
    I will burn up your chariots in smoke;
    a sword will devour your young lions;
    and I will cut off your prey from the earth.
  The voice of your messengers will no longer be heard."

Nahum 3

Judgment Against Nineveh

¹ Woe to the city of blood, completely full of lies, and robbery;
  she is never without victims.
² *Listen!*
    The sound of a whip!
    The noise of a clattering wheel!
    A galloping horse!
    A bounding chariot!
  ³ Charging cavalry! Flashing swords and gleaming spears!

---
a Literally, "the items."
b Literally, "Her hips are trembling."

55

Many are slain; the piles of corpses are heavy.
There is no end to the dead; they stumble over the bodies—
⁴ *all* because of
the wanton lust of the whore *Nineveh*,
the charming one, a mistress of sorceries,
the one who sells nations by her whoring and peoples by her witchcraft.

⁵ The LORD of Armies declares,
"Listen! I am against you!
I will lift up your skirts over your face, and
I will show nations your nakedness and kingdoms your shame.
⁶ I will
pelt you with garbage,
treat you with contempt, and
make you a spectacle.
⁷ Everyone who sees you will recoil from you and say,
'Nineveh is destroyed! Who will grieve for her?'
Where will I seek comforters for you?"

⁸ Are you better than Thebes,
which sits by the Nile, surrounded by water,
whose defense was the waters, and
whose water was her wall?
⁹ Cush and Egypt were her endless might;
Put and Libya were among her allies.
¹⁰ Thebes too has gone into exile;
she has gone into captivity.
Her young children were also dashed to pieces at the head of every street.
They cast lots for her nobles; all her great men were bound with fetters.

¹¹ You also will be drunk.
You will be in hiding.
You also will seek refuge from the enemy.
¹² All your fortresses will be like fig trees with ripe fruit.
If they are shaken, they will fall into the mouth of the eater.

¹³ Consider!
Your troops are *like* women in your midst!
The gates of your land are wide open to your enemies;
fire consumes the bars of your gates.

¹⁴ Draw water for yourself for the siege.
Strengthen your fortifications.
Go into the clay *pits* and tread the mortar *mix*;
strengthen the brickwork!ᵃ
¹⁵ *Despite your efforts,*

---

a Literally, "grab the brick mold."

56

fire will devour you there.

The sword will cut you off.

The enemy will devour you like a swarm of locusts.

There's no hope, even if you multiply yourselves like a swarm of locusts;

yes, even if you multiply yourselves like locusts!

¹⁶ You have increased the number of your merchants, so they outnumber the stars[a] in the sky.

But like locusts, they strip *the land* and fly away.

¹⁷ Your guards are like locusts.

Your officials are like swarms of locusts that settle in the walls on a cold day.

The sun rises and they flee;

no one knows where they are.[b]

¹⁸ O King of Assyria, your shepherds are asleep;

your nobles are lying down.

Your people are scattered on the mountains with no one to gather them.

¹⁹ Nothing can heal you;[c] your wound is incurable.

All who hear the news about you will *joyfully* clap their hands over you,

because who has not suffered under your constant cruelty?[d]

---

a Literally, "so they are more than the stars."
b Literally, "the place where they are is not known."
c Literally, "There is no lessening for your breakdown."
d Literally, "on whom has your cruelty not passed constantly."

Habakkuk

1 *Habakkuk*

¹ The oracle that Habakkuk the prophet saw.

Habakkuk's Cry for Help

² How long, O Lᴏʀᴅ, have I cried for help, but you don't listen?
I cry out to you, "Violence!" but you don't save.
  ³ Why do you show me wickedness and make me see misery?
    Destruction and violence are *right* in front of me.
    There are disputes, and quarrels escalate.
      ⁴ The law is ineffective, and *true* justice never triumphs,*ᵃ*
        for the wicked surround the righteous so that warped justice prevails.*ᵇ*

The Lord Replies: "I Am Raising Up Babylon"

⁵ *Then the Lord replied:*
"Look among the nations! Observe and be completely astounded,
  for I am doing a work in your days that you won't believe when it is told.
  ⁶ For—believe it—
  I am raising up the Babylonians,
    the fast and furious nation
      that marches across the breadth of the land to commandeer
      homes*ᶜ* that are not theirs.
      ⁷ They are terrible and feared;
        their *standard of* justice and honor comes from their *own desire.ᵈ*
          ⁸ Their horses are swifter than leopards and fiercer than wolves *in
          the* evening.
          Their mounted troops gallop and come from afar,*ᵉ* flying like an
          eagle hurrying to devour.
            ⁹ They all come for violence.
              Together they face forward and gather prisoners like sand.
              ¹⁰ They mock kings and ridicule rulers.
                They laugh at every fortress, and they capture them *by* piling up
                earthen *siege ramps.*
                  ¹¹ Then, like the wind, they blow past and go on.
  They are guilty people, whose own strength is their god."

---

a Literally, "never comes out successfully."
b Literally, "justice comes out."
c Literally, "to take possession of dwelling."
d Literally, "their justice and their honor go out from themselves."
e "Mounted troops" appears twice in the text; the second is eliminated to reduce redundancy.

¹² Are you not from everlasting, O LORD my God, my Holy One? We won't die.
> You, LORD, have chosen them to *bring* judgment.
> You, O Rock, have ordained them to correct.
>> ¹³ Your eyes are too pure to look upon evil.
>> You cannot look at wickedness *and approve.*
>>> Why then do you look upon those who deal treacherously *and not act?*
>>> *Why* are you silent when the wicked swallow up people more righteous than they are?
> ¹⁴ You have made people as the fish in the sea,
>> like the creeping things that have no ruler over them.

¹⁵ The Babylonians *are like fishermen who* pull them all up with a hook, drag them in their net, and gather them *into the boat* in their fishing net. Therefore they rejoice and are glad. ¹⁶ They sacrifice to their net and burn incense to their fishing net, *thinking that* because of this, their meal is sumptuous and their food is fattening. ¹⁷ Should they continue emptying their net, slaying nations without sparing *anyone?*

²:¹ I will stand at my post, and
I will station myself on the rampart.
I will watch to see what he will say to me and what I should answer when I am rebuked.

Habakkuk **2**

The Lord Replies: "The Righteous Live by Faith"

² Then the LORD answered me:
> "Write down the *prophetic* vision and carefully record *it* on tablets so that a messenger[a] may run with it. ³ For the vision is still for the future;[b] it speaks of the end[c] and does not lie. Even if it lingers, wait for it, for it will certainly come and will not delay *forever.*

>> ⁴ "Behold, the puffed-up one;[d]
>>> his desires[e] are not upright within him,
>>>> but the righteous one will live by faith.[f]
>>> ⁵ Indeed, wine betrays a proud person so that they are not content.[g]
>>> They widen their appetite like the grave, and
>>>> like death, they are never satisfied.
>>>> They will gather to themselves all the nations and collect for themselves all the peoples.

---

a   Literally, "the one who proclaims it."
b   Literally, "for the appointed time."
c   Literally, "is breathed for the end."
d   Literally, "the swollen one."
e   Or "his soul."
f   Or "by faithfulness."
g   Literally, "so he does not settle."

⁶ "Won't all these nations lift up a taunt against him, a mocking poem or riddle, saying,

> 'Woe to him
> > who multiplies *for himself* what is not his own,
> > who weighs himself down with debt!*a*
> How long *can you keep this up?*'

⁷ Won't your creditors suddenly act—wake up and tun on you?*b* Then you will be their plunder.

> ⁸ For you have plundered many nations, so
> > the peoples who remain will plunder you,
> > because of
> > > the people's blood *you have spilled* and
> > > the violence *you committed* against the land and towns, and
> > > *against* everyone who lives in them.

⁹ "Woe to the one
> who extorts unjust gain for their house,
> > so he can set his nest on high to be saved from harm!*c*
> ¹⁰ You have plotted shame for your own house by cutting off many peoples.
> You have sinned against your own life.
> > ¹¹ Surely the stone of the wall will cry out,
> > and the beams of the woodwork will answer.

¹² "Woe to the one
> who builds a city with bloodshed and establishes a town with injustice!
> > ¹³ Now listen! Isn't it by the LORD of Armies that the people's labor is *nothing but fuel* for the fire and that the nations exhaust themselves for nothing?

¹⁴ For the earth will be filled with the knowledge of the glory of the LORD as the waters cover the sea.

¹⁵ "Woe to the one who gets his friends drunk.*d*
> You mix your poison*e* and make them drunk in order to look at their nakedness.

¹⁶ You will have your fill of shame instead of glory.
> Now you drink too! Let your nakedness*f* be exposed!
> The cup in the LORD's right hand will come around to you, and shame will cover your glory.
> > ¹⁷ For the violence *you have done* to Lebanon will engulf you, and *your* destruction of livestock will terrify you,

---

a Or "and makes himself glorious (*i.e., rich*) with debt" or "with pledges," referring to taking goods others pledged to secure debt.

b Literally, "and oppress you."

c Literally, "from the hand of harm."

d Literally, "gives his neighbors drink" or "makes his neighbor drink."

e Or "You pour out your wineskin."

f Literally, "your circumcision" or "your foreskin."

because of

the people's blood *you have spilled* and

the violence *you committed* against the land and towns and everyone who lives in them.

¹⁸ Of what worth is an idol that a craftsman carves? Or a metal image that teaches a lie?

For the one who created it trusts in his own creation when he makes but mute idols!

¹⁹ "Woe to the one who says,

'Wake up!' to a tree or 'Arise' to a mute stone.

That *idol*ᵃ is your teacher?

Wake up!

The idol is overlaid in gold and silver; there isn't any breath in it at all.

²⁰ For the LORD is in his holy temple.

Let all the earth be silent before him.'"

Habakkuk's Prayer of Praise

¹⁹ᵇ To the music director: *accompanied* by stringed instruments.

¹ A prayer of Habakkuk the prophet in the form of a song.ᵇ

² LORD, I have heard your story;ᶜ

I am in awe of your work, O LORD.

Bring it to life in our time;ᵈ

make it known in our years.

In wrath remember mercy.

Habakkuk's Vision

³ God came from Teman, and the Holy One from Mount Paran.ᵉ   Selah

His splendor covered the heavens, and his praise filled the earth.

⁴ His radiance is like the sun; his raysᶠ *come* from his hand, where his power hides.

⁵ Plague walks before him; pestilence follows at his feet.

⁶ He stood, and the earth shook.ᵍ

He looked, and the nations were startled.

The enduring mountains were shattered, and the ancient hills collapsed; his ways are forever.

⁷ I saw the tents of Cushanʰ in distress, and the curtains of the land of Midian quiver.

---

a Or "That *person*."

b The Hebrew term rendered "in the form of a song," *shigionoth*, is an undefined musical or liturgical term. Perhaps a tune or a musical instrument

c Literally, "heard your hearing."

d Literally, "in the midst of our years."

e Teman and Mount Paran are likely both references to places encountered during the exodus and wilderness wanderings.

f Literally, "the light; his horns."

g Or "and measured the earth."

h "Cushan": an Arabian desert tribe.

Habakkuk's Reflections

⁸ Lᴏʀᴅ, were you angry with the rivers? Angry with the streams?
Or did your fury come against the sea when you rode your horses *and*
chariots of salvation?
  ⁹ You stripped *the cover from* your bow, commissioned[a] your arrows.   Selah
  You split the earth with rivers.
    ¹⁰ Upon seeing you, the mountains writhed.
      A flood of water passed over; the deep gave voice and lifted its waves[b]
      up high.
     ¹¹ The sun and moon stood still in the sky.[c]
     They left
         at the glint of your arrows *flying* and
         at the flash of your lightning-like spear.
¹² In fury you strode through the earth, and in anger you trampled the nations.
¹³ You came out to save your people, to save your anointed one.
      You crushed the head of the house of wickedness, laying him bare
      from base to neck.   Selah
    ¹⁴ You pierced *his* head with his own spear as his warriors stormed in to
    scatter us.
      Their gloating had been as if they were going to secretly devour the poor.
    ¹⁵ You trampled the sea with your horses, *went* through the mighty waters.

Habakkuk's Peace

¹⁶ *When* I heard this, *at first*
    My belly quaked;
    my lips quivered at the thought;[d]
    rottenness spread into my bones, and
    I trembled in place.
Yet I will rest in the day of trouble, *waiting* for the people who will invade us to
rise up.
  ¹⁷ Though the fig tree does not bud and there is no fruit on the vines,
    though the olive harvest fails[e] and the fields yield no food,
    though the sheep are removed from the pen and there are no cattle in
    the stalls,
    ¹⁸ yet I will triumph in the Lᴏʀᴅ;
      I will rejoice in the God of my salvation.
¹⁹ᵃ Gᴏᴅ, the Lord, is my strength.
    He makes my feet like the *feet of a* deer, and
    he leads me onto the heights.

3:19b precedes 3:1 above

---

a Literally, "sworn in with a word." The Hebrew is uncertain.
b Literally, "its hands."
c Literally, "its height" or "its habitation."
d Literally, "at the sound."
e Literally, "work fails."

Zephaniah

¹ The word of the LORD that came to Zephaniah (son of Cushi, son of Gedaliah, son of Amariah, son of Hezekiah) in the days of Josiah son of Amon, king of Judah.

The Day of the Lord for Judah

² The LORD declares,
    "I will surely sweep away everything from the face of the earth.
     ³ I will remove
        people and animals, remove
        the birds of the sky and the fish in the sea, and
        the stumblingblocks along with the wicked.
    I will cut off the human race from the face of the earth," declares the LORD.

⁴ "I will stretch out my hand against Judah and all the residents of Jerusalem.
    I will cut off from that place
        the remnant of Baal,
        the name of the pagan priests along with the priests, ⁵ and
        those
           who bow down on their rooftops to the shining stars,*ᵃ*
           who bow down to and swear by the LORD and *also* Molech,
         ⁶ who turn back from following the LORD,
         who do not seek the LORD nor inquire of him.

⁷ "Be silent before the Lord GOD,
    for the day of the LORD is near!
    The LORD has prepared a sacrifice and consecrated those he has summoned.
⁸ On the day of the LORD's sacrifice I will punish
    the officials,
    the king's sons, and
    all who dress in foreign clothes. ⁹ I will punish
    all who avoid stepping on the threshold*ᵇ* on that day, and
    all who fill their master's house with violence and deceit."

¹⁰ The LORD declares,
    "On that day there will be
        the sound of an outcry from the Fish Gate,*ᶜ*
        wailing from the Second Quarter,*ᵈ* and
        a loud crash from the heights.
     ¹¹ Wail, you who live in Maktesh,
        for all the people of Canaan are destroyed.
        All those who weigh silver are cut off.

---

a Literally, "to the armies of heaven."
b Literally, "who hop over the threshold," a sign of pagan religious observance. See 1 Samuel 5:4–5.
c "Fish Gate": a gate in the Jerusalem wall.
d "Second quarter": A part of Jerusalem, as is "Maktesh" in verse 11.

¹² "At that time I will search out Jerusalem with lamps;
I will punish,
those *complacent ones,*
who settle on their dregs,ᵃ
who say to themselves, 'The Lᴏʀᴅ will neither prosper nor harm.'
¹³ Their wealth will be plundered and their houses destroyed.
They will build houses but not live in them.
They will plant vineyards but not drink their wine."ᵇ

¹⁴ The great day of the Lᴏʀᴅ is near!
It is near and coming very quickly!
There will be a bitter sound on the day of the Lᴏʀᴅ;
warriors will scream there.
¹⁵ That day will be a day of
rage,
distress and affliction,
ruin and desolation,
darkness and shadow,ᶜ
clouds and gloom—
¹⁶ a day for the trumpet and battle cry against the fortified cities and the high
corner towers.

¹⁷ *The Lord says,*
"I will afflict people; they will walk like the blind,
for they have sinned against the Lᴏʀᴅ.
Their blood will be spilled like dust, their corpsesᵈ like dung."

¹⁸ On the day of the Lᴏʀᴅ's rage,
neither their silver nor their gold will be able to save them.
The whole earth will be consumed in the fire of his jealousy,
for he will make a total end, yes, a terrifying one for all who live on the earth.

2 *Zephaniah*

Prophecies Against Judah's Enemies

¹ Gather yourselves together; yes, gather together, O shameless nation,
² before
the decree takes effectᵉ (and the day passes like chaff *on the wind*), before
the burning anger of the Lᴏʀᴅ comes upon you, and before
the day of the Lᴏʀᴅ's wrath comes upon you.
³ Seek the Lᴏʀᴅ, all humble ones of the earth, who observe his ordinances.
Seek righteousness; seek humility;
perhaps you will be hidden on the day of the Lᴏʀᴅ's wrath.

---

a A metaphor for sinful complacency. Picture wine left exposed to air for a long time and deteriorating.
b See Deuteronomy 28:30 and Amos 5:11.
c Literally, "darkness and [another word for darkness]."
d Literally, "their flesh."
e Literally, "is born."

⁴ *The Lord says,*
> "For Gaza will be forsaken and Ashkelon a ruin.
> They will banish Ashdod at midday.
> Ekron will be uprooted.

> ⁵ "Woe to those who live on the shore, *you* nation of Kerethites.
>> The word of the Lord is against you, Canaan, land of the Philistines.
>> I will destroy you, so you cannot be inhabited.
>>> ⁶ The coastal region will become a pastureland with wells^a for shepherds and pens for flocks.
>>>> ⁷ It will belong to the remnant of the house of Judah.
>>>>> They will tend flocks on it and lie down among the *ruined* houses of Ashkelon in the evening,
>>>>>> for the Lord their God will care for them and bring them back from captivity.

⁸ "I have heard the reproaches of Moab and the insults of the Ammonites with which they have berated my people. They have encroached against their borders. ⁹ Therefore, as I live," declares the Lord of Armies, the God of Israel,
> "Surely Moab will become like Sodom and the Ammonites like Gomorrah,
>> a ground overrun with weeds, and salt pits, a ruin forever.
>> The remnant of my people will plunder them.
>> The rest of my nation will possess their property."

¹⁰ This will be their lot
> because of their pride,
>> because they taunted and mocked the people of the Lord of Armies.

¹¹ The Lord will be terrifying to them when he starves all the gods of the earth.
> *All peoples* shall worship him,
>> each in their *own* land, even in the coastlands of the *distant* nations.

¹² *The Lord says,* "You also, Cushites, will be slain by my sword."

¹³ He will turn his hand to the north and destroy Assyria.
> He will make Nineveh a ruin, a waterless place like the wilderness.
>> ¹⁴ Flocks will lie down in the midst of it, all the beasts of the nations.^b
>>> Yes, the owl, even the little-eared owl,^c will roost in the top of its pillars.
>>> Hooting will echo through its windows;
>>> a raven *will rest* on its doorpost;^d and
>>> its cedar work will be ruined.^e

¹⁵ This was the wanton city who dwelt securely, who said in her heart, "I am *the greatest*; there is no one who compares."^f How she has become a ruin, a resting place for beasts. Everyone who passes by her whistles and shakes their fist *in derision.*

---

a Or "with shelters."
b "All the beasts of the nations" would include many animals considered unclean, thus defiling the land.
c Owls were unclean (see Leviticus 11:17).
d From the Septuagint. Masoretic text: "desolation will be at its threshold."
e Literally, "her cedar work will be laid bare."
f Literally, "there is no one besides me."

3 Zephaniah

Judgment Against Jerusalem

¹ Woe to *the city* who is rebellious and polluted, the tyrannical city!
² It does not
    listen to a *rebuking* voice,
    accept correction,
    trust in the Lord, or
    draw near to its God.
³ Its rulers are roaring lions in its midst.
    Its judges are wolves in the nighttime, leaving nothing by morning.[a]
⁴ Its prophets are insolent, treacherous men.
    Its priests have profaned the sanctuary;
        they have done violence to the law.

⁵ The Lord is righteous within it; he does no wickedness.
    He dispenses his justice morning by morning;
        at dawn, he does not fail.
But the ungodly know no shame.

Judgment Against the Nations

⁶ *The Lord says,*
"I have
    cut off nations,
    laid waste to their corner towers, and
    made their streets desolate, with no one passing by.
        Their cities are desolate, without people; no one lives there.
⁷ I said,
    'Surely you will revere me; you will accept correction.
        Then their dwellings would not be destroyed *because* of all the ways[b] I
        punished her.'
    Nevertheless, they got up early to *do their* corrupt deeds.

Purification and Protection of the Lord's Remnant

⁸ "Therefore wait for me, declares the Lord.
    Wait for the day when I get up to testify,
        for I have decided to gather the nations, to assemble the kingdoms,
            for me to pour out my indignation, all my burning anger, on
                them. The fire of my jealousy will consume the whole earth.
⁹ For then I will restore pure speech[c] to the peoples,
    so all of them may call upon the name of the Lord and serve him
        shoulder to shoulder.[d]

---

a   From the Septuagint; the Masoretic text is uncertain.
b   Or "all the times."
c   Or "pure lips."
d   Or "with one accord." Literally, "with one shoulder."

¹⁰ From across the rivers of Cush, my worshipers,ᵃ my scattered people, will
bring me offerings.
¹¹ On that day
> you won't *need to* be ashamed of all the wrongs you have done to me.ᵇ
For at that time
> I will remove from your midst you who rejoice in your pride.
> You will no longer continue arrogantly on my holy mountain.
>> ¹² I will leave *a remnant* in your midst, a people who are humble and poor.
>> They will take refuge in the name of the Lᴏʀᴅ.
>>> ¹³ The remnant of Israel will neither practice injustice nor speak lies.
>>> A deceitful tongue won't be found among them,
>>>> for they will graze *their flocks* and lie down without anyone
>>>> *nearby* who will make them afraid."

¹⁴ Shout for joy, Daughter Zion!
Shout in triumph, O Israel!
Rejoice and exult with all your heart, Daughter Jerusalem!
¹⁵ For
> the Lᴏʀᴅ has taken away your judgments *and* cleared out your enemies.
> The King of Israel, the Lᴏʀᴅ, is among you;
> you will fear evil no more.
¹⁶ In that day it will be said to Jerusalem:
> "Do not fear, O Zion; do not let your hands go limp.
>> ¹⁷ The Lᴏʀᴅ your God is among you, a warrior who saves;
>> he will rejoice over you with joy;
>> he will quiet you with his love;
>> he will rejoice over you with songs of joy."

¹⁸ *The Lord says,*
> "I will remove from you those among you who complain aboutᶜ the
> appointed festivals,ᵈ
>> who have become a burden and reproach to you.ᵉ
>> ¹⁹ See! At that time
>> I will deal with all who oppress you;
>> I will save all the lame and gather up all the banished.
>> I will turn their shame into glory and honor in all the earth.
²⁰ At that time I will bring you *home*, at the time when I gather you. Indeed, I will
give you honor and praise among all the peoples of the earth when I bring
back your captives before your eyes," says the Lᴏʀᴅ.

---

a   Or "my supplicants."
b   Literally, "all your deeds by which you have transgressed against me."
c   Literally, "mourn over."
d   Or "I will remove from you those who mourn over *not celebrating* the appointed festivals. to whom it is
    such a burden and reproach." The Hebrew is uncertain.
e   The Hebrew is uncertain. Or "which has become a burden and reproach to you."

Haggai

A Call to Rebuild the Temple

¹ In the second year of King Darius, in late August,ᵃ the word of the LORD came through Haggai the prophet to Zerubbabel the governor of Judah, the son of Shealtiel, and Joshua the high priest, the son of Jehozadak.

² The LORD of Armies says this:
> "These people say,
>> 'The time has not come for the temple of the LORD to be rebuilt.'
> ³ But I say,ᵇ
>> ⁴ 'Is it time for you yourselves to live in your paneled houses, while this temple is a ruin?'"

⁵ Now the LORD of Armies says this:
> "Think about your ways!
>> ⁶ You have sown much seed
>>> but harvested little.
>> You have eaten,
>>> but you are not satisfied.
>> You have drunk
>>> but not enough to get drunk.ᶜ
>> You put on clothes
>>> but are not warm.
>> You earn wages
>>> but *put* them in a purse with holes."
> ⁷ So the LORD of Armies says,
>> "Think about your ways!
>>> ⁸ Go up to the mountains and bring wood and rebuild the temple, so I will be pleased with it and be glorified," says the LORD.

>> ⁹ "You have expected much,
>>> but look, there was little.
>> You brought it to your house,
>>> but I blew it away.
>> Why?" asks the LORD of Armies.
>>> "Because of my temple, which is a ruin, while each of you cares forᵈ your own house.

---

a Literally, "on the first day of the sixth month"; about 538 BC.
b Literally, "Then the word of the LORD came through Haggai the prophet, saying."
c Literally, "but no drunkenness."
d Literally, "each of you runs to."

¹⁰ Therefore, because of you,
   the skies have withheld their dew, and the earth has withheld its produce.
   ¹¹ I proclaimed a drought on
      the land and the mountains,
      the grain, new wine, and olive oil—everything the soil produces;
      people, livestock, and everything your hands produce."

¹² Zerubbabel son of Shealtiel, Joshua son of Jehozadak, the high priest, and all the remnant of the people listened to the voice of the Lord their God and to the words of Haggai the prophet, since the Lord their God had sent him. Then the people showed proper respect to*ᵃ* the Lord.

¹³ Then Haggai, the Lord's messenger, delivered the Lord's message to the people: "I am with you," declares the Lord.

¹⁴ Then the Lord stirred up the spirits of Zerubbabel the governor of Judah, son of Shealtiel, and Joshua the high priest, the son of Jehozadak, and all the remnant of the people. They came and worked on the temple of the Lord of Armies, their God, ¹⁵ in mid-September of the second year of King Darius.ᵇ

Haggai **2**

Blessings for Rebuilding the Temple

¹ *A month later,* in mid-October,ᶜ the word of the Lord came to Haggai the prophet:
   ² "Say to Zerubbabel son of Shealtiel, the governor of Judah, and to Joshua the
      high priest, the son of Jehozadak, and the remnant of the people,
      ³ 'Who is left from among you who has seen this temple in its former glory?
         How do you see it now?
         Doesn't it look like nothing in your opinion?ᵈ
   ⁴ But now, declares the Lord,
      be strong, Zerubbabel,
      be strong, Joshua the high priest, son of Jehozadak.
      Be strong, all you people of the land, says the Lord of Armies.
      Do it,
         for I am with you, declares the Lord of Armies.
            ⁵ As for the promise that I made you when you came out of Egypt,
               my Spirit is still among you.
      Do not fear! ⁶ For the Lord of Armies says this:
         Once again, in a little while,
            I will shake the skies, the earth, the sea, and the dry land.
               ⁷ I will shake all the nations,
                  and they will come *with* the wealth of all the nations.
            I will fill this temple with glory,' says the Lord of Armies.

---

a Literally, "the people feared."
b Literally, "on the twenty-fourth day of the sixth month"; about 538 BC.
c Literally, "on the twenty-first day of the seventh month"; about 538 BC.
d Literally, "in your eyes."

⁸ 'The silver is mine, and the gold is mine,' declares the Lord of Armies.

⁹ 'The glory of this latter temple will exceed that of the former, says the Lord of Armies.

I will grant peace in this place, declares the Lord of Armies.'"

¹⁰ *Two months later,* in mid-December in the second year of *King* Darius,*ᵃ* the word of the Lord came to Haggai the prophet: ¹¹ "The Lord of Armies says this:

Ask the priests *this about* the law: ¹² If someone takes consecrated meat in their pocket*ᵇ* and the pocket touches bread, boiled food, wine, olive oil, or any other food, will it become holy?"

The priests answered, "No."

¹³ Then Haggai asked, "If someone who is unclean from *touching* a corpse touches any of these, will it be unclean?"

The priests answered, "It will be unclean."

¹⁴ Then Haggai said,

"So is this people and this nation before me, declares the Lord. So are all the works of their hands. Whatever they offer there is unclean.

¹⁵ "And now, think about it from this day on: Consider *how bleak life was* before *a single* stone was placed on another *to rebuild* the Lord's temple— ¹⁶ back when*ᶜ* one would come to a grain pile of twenty *measures,* and it would be *only* ten, or come to a wine vat to draw out fifty measures, and it would be *only* twenty. ¹⁷ I struck you and everything you produced*ᵈ* with scorching wind, mildew, and hail, but you did not *turn* to me," declares the Lord.

¹⁸ "Think about it from this day onward, from *today,* the middle of December, the day the Lord's temple was founded. Think about it: ¹⁹ Is the seed still in the barn? Neither the grapevine, the fig tree, the pomegranate, nor the olive tree have yet borne fruit. But from this day *on* I will bless *you.*"

²⁰ The word of the Lord came to Haggai a second time on that same day:*ᵉ*

²¹ "Tell Zerubbabel governor of Judah that
I will
shake the heavens and the earth,
²² overthrow thrones of kingdoms and destroy the power of foreign kingdoms,*ᶠ* and
overthrow chariots and their riders—
horses will go down with their riders, each by his fellow soldier's sword.*ᵍ*

²³ "On that day, declares the Lord of Armies, I will take you, Zerubbabel son of Shealtiel, my servant, declares the Lord, and make you like a signet ring, for I have chosen you, declares the Lord of Armies."

---

a   Literally, "on the twenty-fourth day of the ninth month." And verse 18. About 538 BC.
b   Literally, "in the wing of their garment."
c   Literally, "from that time."
d   Literally, "and every work of your hands."
e   Literally, "on the twenty-fourth day of the month."
f   Literally, "of the kingdoms of nations."
g   Literally, "by his brother's sword."

Zechariah

Part I. Dated Prophecies

¹ In late fall*ᵃ* of the second year of *King* Darius, the word of the Lᴏʀᴅ came to the prophet Zechariah son of Berekiah, son of Iddo.

A Call to Repentance

² "The Lᴏʀᴅ was very angry with your ancestors. ³ Therefore tell the people, the Lᴏʀᴅ of Armies says this:

'Return to me, declares the Lᴏʀᴅ of Armies, and I will return to you.'
The Lᴏʀᴅ of Armies has spoken.
⁴ Do not be like your ancestors,
to whom the earlier prophets called out, 'The Lᴏʀᴅ of Armies says this:
Turn from your evil ways and deeds'—but they did not listen or pay
attention to me, declares the Lᴏʀᴅ.
⁵ *As for* your ancestors, where are they *now*? Or
as for the prophets, do they live forever?
⁶ Didn't my words and my statutes, which I commanded to my servants
the prophets, overtake your ancestors?
So they repented and said, 'The Lᴏʀᴅ of Armies has treated us
according to our ways and deeds, just as he determined to do.'"

Eight Visions

⁷ In mid-February of the second year of *King* Darius,*ᵇ* the word of the Lᴏʀᴅ came to the prophet Zechariah son of Berekiah, son of Iddo. ⁸ I saw this in a vision.*ᶜ*

Vision 1. A Man Riding a Red Horse Among Myrtle Trees

To my surprise, *there was* a man mounted on a red horse! He was standing among the myrtle trees in the ravine, and behind him were red, brown, and white horses. ⁹ I said, "What are these, my lord?"

The angel who spoke to me replied, "I will show you what they are."

¹⁰ The man who was standing among the myrtle trees said, "They are those whom the Lᴏʀᴅ has sent to patrol the earth."

¹¹ They said to the angel of the Lᴏʀᴅ who was standing among the myrtle trees, "We have been patrolling the earth, and indeed, the entire earth is peaceful and quiet."

---

a   Literally, "In the eighth month." About 538 BC.
b   Literally, "On the twenty-fourth day of the eleventh month, the month of Shebat." About 537 BC.
c   Literally, "I saw at night."

¹² The angel of the Lord said, "O Lord of Armies, how long will you refuse to have compassion on Jerusalem and the cities of Judah, with whom you have been angry for these seventy years?"

¹³ The Lord spoke pleasant and comforting words to the angel who spoke to me.

¹⁴ The angel speaking to me said,
>"Call out, 'the Lord of Armies says this:
>>I am jealous for Jerusalem, very jealous for Zion.
>>¹⁵ I am enraged against the complacent nations against whom I used to be *only* a little angry. They intensified the disaster.*ᵃ*
>
>¹⁶ Therefore the Lord says this:
>>I will return to Jerusalem with compassion.
>>>My temple will be rebuilt within her, declares the Lord of Armies, and a measuring line will be stretched over Jerusalem.'

¹⁷ "Call out yet again, 'the Lord of Armies says this:
>My cities will again overflow with prosperity;
>the Lord will again comfort Zion and again choose Jerusalem.'"

Vision 2. Four Horns and Four Craftsmen

¹⁸ I looked up, and to my surprise, there were four horns.*ᵇ* ¹⁹ I asked the angel who was speaking with me, "What are these?"

He replied, "These are the horns that scattered Judah, Israel, and Jerusalem."

²⁰ Then the Lord showed me four blacksmiths.*ᶜ* ²¹ I said, "What are these coming to do?"

He replied, "These are the horns that scattered Judah so *badly* that no one could lift up their head; but the craftsmen have come to terrify them, to throw down the horns of the nations who have lifted up their horns against the land of Judah to scatter its *people*."

2 Zechariah

Vision 3. A Man with a Measuring Line

¹ I looked up *again*, and there before me, a man *stood* with a measuring line in his hand. ² So I asked, "Where are you going?"

He replied, "To measure Jerusalem, to see what its width and length are."

³ Suddenly, the angel who was speaking with me went out, and another angel came out to meet him. ⁴ He said to him,
>"Run, tell that young man, 'Jerusalem will be inhabited without walls, because so many people and livestock are in it. ⁵ As for me, I will be a wall of fire all around her, declares the Lord, and I will be the glory within her.'"

---

a   Literally, "They helped the evil."

b   In the following material, "horns" symbolize power and arrogance.

c   Literally, "craftsmen." But the context (powerful horns that would probably be made of metal) indicates that they were blacksmiths.

⁶ *The angel continued,*

"Listen to me! Flee from the northern land, declares the Lord, for I have dispersed you like the four winds of heaven, declares the Lord. ⁷ Listen, Zion! Escape, you who are living in Daughter Babylon!" ⁸ For the Lord of Armies says this: "After glory*ᵃ* has sent me to the nations who plundered you—for whoever touches you touches the apple of his eye— ⁹ then watch! I will wave my hand over them, and they will become plunder for their slaves. Then you will know that the Lord of Armies has sent me.

¹⁰ "Shout aloud and rejoice, Daughter Zion, because look— I am coming.
  I will live among you, declares the Lord.
  ¹¹ Many nations will join themselves to the Lord on that day,
    and they will become my people.
  I will live among you,
    and you will know that the Lord of Armies has sent me to you.
  ¹² The Lord will possess Judah as his portion in the holy land, and
    he will again choose Jerusalem.
¹³ Be silent, all flesh, in the Lord's presence! For he has roused himself from his holy dwelling."

Zechariah 3

Vision 4. Clean Garments for the High Priest

¹ He showed me Joshua the high priest standing before the angel of the Lord and Satan standing at his right hand accusing him. ² The Lord said to the Accuser,ᵇ "The Lord rebuke you, Satan! The Lord, who has chosen Jerusalem, rebuke you! Isn't this man a burning stick snatched from the fire?"

³ Now Joshua was dressed in filthyᶜ robes and standing before the angel. ⁴ The angel said to those standing before him, "Remove the filthy robes from him." And he said to Joshua, "See! I have taken your sins away.ᵈ I will dress you in fine robes."

⁵ Then I said, "Let them put a clean turban on his head." So they put a clean turban on his head and dressed him in *clean* robes, while the angel of the Lord stood by.
  ⁶ Then the angel of the Lord gave Joshua this charge:ᵉ
    ⁷ "The Lord of Armies says this:
      'If you walk in my ways and keep my charge,
      then
        you will governᶠ my house and oversee my courts.
        I will give you free accessᵍ among those standing *here.*

---

a "After glory" may (1) refer to the pursuit of glory (therefore, "For my own glory"), (2) refer to a time period (e.g., after the glory promised to Israel has been realized), or (3) be a term for God (therefore, "After the Glorious One").
b Or transliterated, "Satan."
c Literally, "robes soiled with excrement."
d Literally, "I have made your iniquities pass from above you."
e Literally, "bore witness to Joshua."
f Literally, "will judge."
g Literally, "places to walk."

⁸ Listen, High Priest Joshua,

> you and your companions who sit before you are signs *of things to come.*

Watch!

> I am bringing my servant, the Branch.

⁹ See,

> the stone I have placed before Joshua—
>> on one stone are seven facets.^{*a*}
>> See! I am engraving an inscription on it, declares the Lord of Armies, and I will remove the iniquity of that land in a single day. ¹⁰ In that day, declares the Lord of Armies, everyone will invite their neighbor *to sit* beneath their own vine and fig tree.' "

4 *Zechariah*

Vision 5. A Gold Lampstand and Two Olive Trees

¹ The angel who had been speaking to me returned and wakened me like a man who is wakened from his sleep. ² He asked me, "What do you see?"

I said, "I am looking, and there *I see*

> a solid gold lampstand with
>> a bowl on top,
>> seven lamps on it,
>> seven spouts for the lamps that are on top of it, ³ and
> two olive trees by it,
>> one to the right of the bowl and one to the left."

⁴ Then I said to the angel who was speaking to me, "What are these, my lord?"

⁵ He replied, "Don't you know what they are?"

I said, "No, my lord."

⁶ He replied, "This is the word of the Lord to Zerubbabel:

> 'Not by might nor by power but by my Spirit,' says the Lord of Armies.
> ⁷ Who are you, great mountain? Before Zerubbabel you will become a plain. He will bring out the *temple* capstone^{*b*} to shouts of 'God bless it! God bless it!' "^{*c*}

⁸ The word of the Lord came to me *also*:

> ⁹ "Zerubbabel's hands have laid this temple's foundations, and his hands will finish it. Then you will know that the Lord of Armies has sent me to you. ¹⁰ For who despised the day of small things? These seven will rejoice when they see the plumb line^{*d*} in Zerubbabel's hand. These *facets represent* the eyes of the Lord that range throughout the earth."

---

a Literally, "seven eyes."
b "Capstone": the final stone to be put in place.
c Literally, "Grace to it! Grace to it!"
d "Plumb line": from the Septuagint; Masoretic text is uncertain.

[11] I asked him, "What are these two olive trees on the right and left of the lampstand?" [12] Then I spoke to him a second time, "What are the two olive branches that are beside the two golden pipes that pour out golden *oil* from themselves?"

[13] He answered me, "Don't you know what they are?"

I replied, "No, my lord."

[14] He said, "These *represent* the two anointed ones who stand before the Lord of all the earth."

Zechariah 5

Vision 6. A Flying Scroll

[1] I turned, raised my eyes, and looked up, and there was a flying scroll! [2] The angel said to me, "What do you see?"

I replied, "I see a flying scroll. Its length is thirty feet and its width is fifteen feet."*a*

[3] He said to me,

"This is the curse that has gone out on the face of all the land, for everyone who steals will be purged away according to what is written on one side,*b* and all who swear *falsely* will be purged away according to what is written on the other side. [4] 'I will send it out, declares the Lord of Armies, and it will come to the house of the thief and the house of the one who swears falsely by my name. It will remain in that house and destroy it, *including* its timbers and stones.'"

Vision 7. A Woman in a Basket

[5] The angel who was speaking to me came forward and said to me, "Look up and see what this is that's coming out."

[6] I replied, "What is it?"

He said, "This is a measuring basket*c* that is coming out." Then he said, "This is *filled with* their iniquity in all the land."*d* [7] Surprisingly, the lead cover was lifted up, and there was a woman sitting inside the basket! [8] He said, "This is Wickedness." He pushed her into the middle of the basket and threw the lead weight on its opening.

[9] Then I raised my eyes and looked, and in fact, two women were coming out, and wind was in their wings. They had wings like those of a stork. They lifted up the basket between earth and sky. [10] I asked the angel who was speaking with me, "Where are they taking the basket?"

[11] He answered, "To build a temple for Babylon*e* in the land of Shinar. When it is prepared, the basket will be set there in its place."*f*

---

a   Literally, "twenty cubits long and ten cubits wide."
b   Literally, "from this *side*," and again at the end of the verse.
c   Literally, "This is an ephah." And in subsequent verses in this section. An ephah is a basket measure.
d   From the Septuagint; Masoretic text: "This is their eye."
e   Literally, "for her."
f   Or "on its base."

Vision 8. Four Chariots

[1] Again I turned, raised my eyes, and looked, and right before me four chariots were coming out from between two mountains, mountains of bronze! [2] Red horses *pulled* the first chariot, and black horses *pulled* the second. [3] White horses *pulled* the third, and dappled horses *pulled* the fourth—all of them were powerful. [4] I said to the angel who was speaking with me, "What are these, my lord?"

[5] The angel replied,

"These are the four spirits[a] of heaven, going out from the presence of[b] the Lord of all the earth. [6] The one with the black horses is going out to the land of the north, the one with the white horses is going after them, and the one with the dappled horses is going toward the south." [7] When the powerful horses[c] went out, they were eager to walk and rove throughout the earth. He said to them, "Go, rove throughout the earth." So they did. [8] Then he cried out and said to me, "Look at the ones going to the land of the north. They have given my Spirit rest in the land of the north."

Part 2. Direct Instructions and a Prediction

[9] The word of the LORD came to me:

[10] "Take *the gift* from the exiles, *from* Heldai,[d] Tobijah, and Jedaiah (who have arrived from Babylon), and go that same day to the house of Josiah son of Zephaniah. [11] Take the silver and gold, make a crown, and put it on the head of Joshua the high priest, son of Jehozadak.

[12] "Tell him, 'The LORD of Armies says this:

Look at the man whose name is Branch. He will branch out from his place. He will rebuild the temple of the LORD. [13] He is the one who will rebuild the temple of the LORD, and he will bear splendor and sit and rule on his throne. He will be a priest on his throne, and there will be no conflict[e] between the two *offices he holds*.

[14] The crown will be *given into the care* of Heldai, Tobijah, Jedaiah, and Hen (a.k.a. Josiah) son of Zephaniah as a memorial in the LORD's temple. [15] Those who are far away will come and build the LORD's temple. Then you will know that the LORD of Armies has sent me to you. It will take place if you diligently obey the voice of the LORD your God."

---

a   Or "four winds."
b   Literally, "from standing before."
c   Literally, "powerful ones."
d   From the Syriac text; Masoretic text: "Helem." It is unclear whether the gift was from these three persons or brought from the exiles by them.
e   Literally, "there will be peaceful counsel."

Carry Out Meaningful Actions, Not Meaningless Fasting and Mourning

¹ In early December*ᵃ* of the fourth year of King Darius,*ᵇ* the word of the Lᴏʀᴅ came to Zechariah. ² *The people of* Bethel had sent Sharezer and Regem-Melech and their men to make seek the Lᴏʀᴅ's favor,*ᶜ* ³ asking the priests and the prophets who were at the Lᴏʀᴅ's temple, "Should I weep and abstain in the fifth *month* just like I have done for these many years?"

⁴ The word of the Lᴏʀᴅ of Armies came to me:
⁵ "Ask all the people of the land and the priests,
'When you fasted and wept on the fifth and seventh *months*ᵈ these seventy years,
were you actually fasting for me?
⁶ When you ate and drank,
weren't you eating and drinking for yourselves?
⁷ Aren't *these* the *same* words the Lᴏʀᴅ proclaimed through*ᵉ* the former prophets, when Jerusalem was inhabited and prosperous with the cities around it, and the Negev and the foothills were settled?'"

⁸ The word of the Lᴏʀᴅ came to Zechariah:
⁹ "The Lᴏʀᴅ of Armies has said,
'Dispense true justice. Act with loyal love and compassion, each one to their neighbor.
¹⁰ Do not oppress the widow or the orphan, the stranger or the poor.
Let no one plan evil against their brother or sister in their heart.'
¹¹ But they
refused to pay attention;
turned their backs*ᶠ* and
stopped their ears from hearing. ¹² They
made their hearts like flint,*ᵍ*
so they would not obey the law nor the messages that the Lᴏʀᴅ of Armies sent by his Spirit through the former prophets.
Therefore great wrath poured out from the Lᴏʀᴅ of Armies.

¹³ "And it happened, just as *before*: I called, but they did not listen;
so *it is*: They called, but I would not listen, says the Lᴏʀᴅ of Armies.

¹⁴ "I scattered them with a whirlwind among all the nations whom they have not known. The land was made desolate behind them so that no one passed through it or returned. They made the pleasant land desolate."

---

a Literally, "on the fourth day of the ninth month, Kislev."
b About 536 BC.
c Literally, "to soften the face of the Lᴏʀᴅ."
d Jews mourned the destruction of the temple by Nebuchadnezzar in the fifth month, and they fasted in the seventh month.
e Literally, "proclaimed by the hand of"; also in verse 12.
f Literally, "they gave a stubborn shoulder."
g "Flint": a hard, dark quartz.

¹ The word of the Lord of Armies came:

² "The Lord of Armies says this:

'I am extremely jealous for Zion's *love*; I am jealous with great wrath.'

³ The Lord says,

'I will return to *Mount* Zion.
I will dwell in the midst of Jerusalem.
Jerusalem will be called
the City of Truth and
the mountain of the Lord of Armies,
the Holy Mountain.'

⁴ "The Lord of Armies says this:

'Old men and women will again sit in Jerusalem's squares, each with a staff in their hand because of their age.ᵃ ⁵ The squares of the cities will also be filled with boys and girls playing there.'

⁶ "The Lord of Armies says this:

'If this is too marvelous in the sight of the remnant of this people in those days, will it also be too marvelous in my eyes? declares the Lord of Armies.'

⁷ "The Lord of Armies says this: 'Listen!

I will save my people
from the land of the east and the land of the west.
⁸ I will bring them in, and
they will live in the midst of Jerusalem.
They will be my people, and
I will be their God in truth and righteousness.'

⁹ "The Lord of Armies says this:

'Strengthen your hands,
you who in these days hear the words of the prophetsᵇ
(*those* who *were present*ᶜ on the day that the foundation of the house of the Lord of Armies was laid)
so that the temple may be built.
¹⁰ For before those days, there was no wage for people nor hire for animals. There was no peace for those who went in or out because of the foe. I set all people, everyone, against his neighbor. ¹¹ But I won't treat the remnant of this people as *I did* in the past,ᵈ declares the Lord of Armies.

---

a Literally, "their many days."
b Literally, "to the words from the mouth of the prophets."
c Or "who *spoke*."
d Literally, "as in former days."

¹² For I will sow peace;
>
> the vine will bear its fruit;
>
> the land will give its yield;
>
> the skies will give their dew.

I will cause the remnant of this people to inherit all these things. ¹³ Just as you were a curse among the nations, O house of Judah and house of Israel, so will I save you and you will be a blessing. Do not fear; strengthen your hands!'

¹⁴ "For the LORD of Armies says this:

> 'Just as I determined to bring disaster to you when your ancestors aroused my wrath, says the LORD of Armies, and I have not relented, ¹⁵ so will I again determine in these days to do good to Jerusalem and the people of Judah. Do not fear!

¹⁶ "'These are the things you should do:

> Everyone speak the truth to their neighbor.
>
> Judge with truth, justice, and peace in your gates.

¹⁷ "'Do not plot evil against each other in your hearts.
>
> Do not love false oaths,
>
>> for I hate all these things, declares the LORD.'"

¹⁸ The word of the LORD of Armies came to me:

¹⁹ "The LORD of Armies says this:

> 'The fasts of the fourth, fifth, seventh, and tenth months will be a joy to the people of Judah; they will be happy occasions with rejoicing. So love truth and peace!'

²⁰ "The LORD of Armies says this:

> 'Peoples and inhabitants of many cities will yet come.

²¹ The residents of one will come to another and say,

> "We will certainly go up to petition*a* the LORD and to seek the LORD of Armies. I also will go."

²² Many peoples and powerful nations will come to seek the LORD of Armies in Jerusalem and petition the LORD.'

²³ "The LORD of Armies says this:

> 'In those days people from all languages and nations will grab the hem of a Jew's *garment* and say, 'Let us go with you, for we have heard that God is with you.'"

---

a   Literally, "and soften the face of"; also in verse 22.

Part 3. Undated Prophecies

9 *Zechariah*

Judgment on Syria, Phoenicia, and Philistia

[1] A prophecy:[a]
The word of the Lord is
against the land of Hadrach and
will come to rest on Damascus
(for the eyes of all people and all the tribes of Israel are on the Lord) [2] and
also on Hamath, which borders it,
and Tyre and Sidon, though they are very skillful.[b]
[3] Tyre has built a stronghold for herself and piled up silver like dust and
gold like mud in the streets. [4] Watch! The Lord will dispossess her. He will
destroy her power on the sea, and she will be devoured by fire.

[5] Ashkelon will see it and be afraid.
Gaza will writhe in great agony, and
Ekron[c] as well,
because her expectation has been dashed.
A king has perished from Gaza, and Ashkelon won't be inhabited.

[6] *The Lord says,*
"A mixed people[d] will live in Ashdod;
I will cut off the pride of the Philistines.
[7] I will remove the blood from their mouths and the disgusting things from
between their teeth.
Then they also will be a remnant worshiping our God.[e]
They will be like a clan in Judah, and Ekron will be like the Jebusites.
[8] But I will encamp around my temple because of an army, one that goes and
returns. No oppressor will overrun my people[f] anymore, for now I have seen
with my eyes."

[9] Shout with abounding joy, Daughter Zion!
Cry aloud, Daughter Jerusalem!
Look! Your king is coming to you.
He is righteous and victorious,
humble and riding on a donkey,
on a colt, the foal of a donkey.

---

a   Literally, "A burden."
b   Or "are very wise."
c   Ashkelon, Gaza, and Ekron were three important Canaanite cities.
d   "Mixed people": whether this means a Jewish parent and a gentile one or some other mixture is uncertain.
e   Literally, "a remnant to our God."
f   Literally, "pass through them."

¹⁰ He*a* will cut off chariots from Ephraim and war horses from Jerusalem.
The battle bow will be broken.
He will proclaim peace to the nations, and
his reign will extend
from sea to sea and from the Euphrates River to the ends of the earth.

¹¹ *The Lord says,*
"As for you,
I will set your prisoners free from the waterless pit,
because of the blood of my covenant with you.
¹² Return to the stronghold, you prisoners who have the hope. Moreover,
today I am announcing that I will restore double to you.
¹³ For
I will bend Judah like my bow and fill it with Ephraim.
I will rouse your sons, O Zion, against your sons, O Greece.
I will make you like a warrior's sword.
¹⁴ The LORD will appear over them.
His arrow will come out like lightning, and
the Lord GOD will sound the trumpet and march in the
storm winds of the south.
¹⁵ The LORD of Armies will defend them.
They will
devour and subdue with slingstones,
drink and be uproarious as with wine, and
be full like a *sacrificial* basin, *drenched* like the corners of the altar.
¹⁶ The LORD their God will deliver his people on that day
as *a shepherd saves* a flock,*b*
for they are like jewels in a crown, sparkling in his land.
¹⁷ O what attractiveness and beauty will be theirs! Grain will
make their young men flourish, and new wine *will make* their
young women *flourish.*"

Zechariah **10**

Denouncement of Judah's Foreign Rulers

¹ Ask for showers from the LORD at the time of the spring rain,
from the LORD who makes the storm clouds.
And he will give showers of rain and vegetation in the field to everyone.

² For the household gods encourage*c* iniquity, and the diviners see lying visions
and tell false dreams.
They give useless comfort.
Therefore the people wander like sheep;
they are afflicted for lack of a shepherd.

---

a   From the Septuagint; Masoretic text: "I."
b   Or "will deliver them as the flock of his people."
c   Literally, "speak."

³ *The Lord says,*
  "My anger is aroused against the shepherds;
  I will punish the leaders,ᵃ
    for the Lord of Armies has visited his flock, the people of Judah.
  I will make them like a majestic horse in battle.
⁴ From them will come
    the cornerstone,
    the tent peg,
    the bow for battle, and
    every ruler—*all of them* together.
⁵ They will be like warriors, trampling down *the foe* in the muddy streets in
  battle. They will fight, for the Lord will be with them. They will put *enemy*
  horsemen to shame.

⁶ "I will strengthen the people of Judah and save the descendants of Joseph;
  I will bring them back, because I have compassion on them.
    They will be as though I had never rejected them,
      for I, the Lord their God, will answer them.
  ⁷ Ephraim will be like a warrior;
    their hearts will rejoice as with wine,
      and their descendants will see and rejoice.
    Their hearts will rejoice in the Lord.
⁸ I will whistle for them and gather them,
    for I have redeemed them.
    They will be as numerous as they were before.
⁹ Though I scatter them among the peoples, they will remember me in
  faraway lands.
  They and their children will survive and return.
    ¹⁰ I will bring them back from Egypt and gather them from Assyria;
      I will bring them to Gilead and Lebanon,
        until no *room* is found for them.

¹¹ "They will pass through the sea of trouble.
  He will
    hold backᵇ the waves of the sea,
    dry up all the depths of the Nile, and
    bring down the pride of Assyria.
  The scepter of Egypt will disappear.

¹² "I will strengthen them in the Lord.
    They will walk about in his name, declares the Lord."

---

a Literally, "their male goats."
b Literally, "will strike."

The Role of the Shepherd

¹ Open your doors, O Lebanon, that fire may devour your cedars.
² Wail, O cypress,
> for the cedar has fallen,
> because the glorious trees have been destroyed.
> Wail, oaks of Bashan,
> for the dense forest has come down.
³ The voices of the shepherds are wailing,
> because their rich pasture*ᵃ* is ruined.
> The voices of the young lions are roaring,
> because the lush thickets*ᵇ* of the Jordan *valley* are ruined.

⁴ The Lᴏʀᴅ my God said,
> "Tend the flock *marked* for slaughter. ⁵ Their buyers slaughter them and are not punished. Their sellers say, 'Blessed be the Lᴏʀᴅ, for I have become rich!' Their own shepherds have no pity on them. ⁶ For I won't have pity anymore on those who live in the land," declares the Lᴏʀᴅ. "Watch! I am giving everyone into the hands of their neighbor and their king. They will beat the land to pieces, and I won't rescue *anyone* from their hands."

⁷ So I tended the flock *marked* for slaughter, the inferior ones of the flock. I took two staffs for myself and called one Favor and the other Union, and I tended the flock. ⁸ I kicked out three shepherds in one month. But I grew impatient with the flock, and the sheep detested me.*ᶜ* ⁹ So I said, "I will not tend you. The dying will die, the disappearing will disappear,*ᵈ* and the ones who are left will devour one another's flesh." ¹⁰ I took my staff, *named* Favor, and cut it to pieces to break the covenant I had made with all the peoples. ¹¹ It was broken on that day, and the afflicted of the flock who were watching me knew that my action was *a picture of* the word of the Lᴏʀᴅ.*ᵉ* ¹² I said to them, "If it is good in your opinion, give me my wages; if not, keep it." So they weighed out thirty *pieces* of silver for my wages.

¹³ The Lᴏʀᴅ said to me, "Throw it to the potter"—that magnificent price*ᶠ* at which I was valued by them! So I took the thirty pieces of silver and threw them to the potter at the temple. ¹⁴ Then I cut my second staff, *named* Union, to pieces to break the family bond between Judah and Israel.

---

a Literally, "their glory."
b Literally, "the pride."
c Literally, "My soul was short with them, and also their souls disdained me."
d Or "the perishing will perish."
e Literally, "knew that it was the word of the Lᴏʀᴅ."
f "Magnificent price": a sarcastic statement belittling the small value placed on his work.

^{15} Then the Lord said to me,

"Take up the tools of a foolish shepherd again. ^{16} For in fact, I am raising up a shepherd in the land who will not care for the perishing, look for the scattered, heal the injured, nor sustain the healthy,^{a} but will devour the flesh of the fat *sheep* and tear off their hooves.

^{17} "Woe to the worthless shepherd, the one who deserts the sheep!
May a sword pierce^b his arm and right eye!
May his arm be totally withered and his right eye completely blinded!"

12 Zechariah

The Restoration of Jerusalem

^{1} A prophecy:^{c} the word of the Lord concerning Israel. The Lord says this:

The one who
stretched out the heavens,
founded the earth, and
created the spirit of a person,^{d} speaks.

^{2} "Hear this!
I am going to make Jerusalem a cup that causes all the nations around them to reel. When Jerusalem is besieged, the siege will be against Judah as well.
^{3} "On that day^e
I will make Jerusalem a heavy stone for all the peoples;
all who lift it will be severely injured.
And all the nations of the earth will be gathered against her!
^{4} I will strike," declares the Lord, "every horse with confusion and its rider with madness.
But I will watch over^f the people of Judah, while I strike every horse of the peoples with blindness. ^{5} The clans of Judah will think, 'The residents of Jerusalem are strong for us through the Lord of Armies, their God.'
^{6} I will make the clans of Judah like a firepot in a woodpile, like a flaming torch among sheaves.
They will devour to the right and the left all the surrounding peoples,
but *the people of* Jerusalem will continue to live in their place,
in Jerusalem.
^{7} The Lord will rescue the homes of Judah first
so that the glory of David's house and of the residents of Jerusalem will not be greater than Judah's.

---

a Literally, "the one standing."
b Literally, "sword will be on."
c Literally, "A burden."
d Or "people's breath within them."
e "On that day" is repeated at the start of verses 4, 6, 8, 9, 11; 13:1, 2, 4.
f Literally, "I will open my eyes toward."

⁸ "The Lord will defend the residents of Jerusalem.
>
> The feeblest of them will be like David in that day, and the house of David
> will be like God, like the angel of the Lord *going* before them.

⁹ "I will seek to destroy all the nations that invade Jerusalem.
>
> ¹⁰ I will pour out on the house of David and on the residents of Jerusalem a
> spirit of grace and supplication, and they will gaze upon me, the one they
> have pierced. They will mourn for him like the mourning for an only child
> and weep bitterly for him as though weeping *in mourning* for a firstborn.

¹¹ "In that day there will be great mourning in Jerusalem,
>
> like the mourning of Hadad Rimmon in the plain of Megiddo.

¹² The land will mourn, every family by itself:
>
> the family of the house of David by itself
>> and their wives by themselves;
>
> the family of the house of Nathan by itself
>> and their wives by themselves;
>
> ¹³ the family of the house of Levi by itself
>> and their wives by themselves;
>
> the family of the Shimeites*ᵃ* by itself
>> and their wives by themselves;
>
> ¹⁴ and all the families that remain, each by itself,
>> and their wives by themselves.

Zechariah **13**

¹ "A fountain will be opened for the house of David and the residents of
Jerusalem for sin and impurity.

² "I will cut off the names of the idols from the land, declares the Lord of Armies.
> They won't be remembered anymore.

I will also remove the *false* prophets and the spirit of uncleanness from
the land.

> ³ If one of them should prophesy again, that person's parents*ᵇ* will say to
> *their child,* 'You shall not live, for you have spoken lies in the name of the
> Lord.' The parents will stab their child when he prophesies.

> ⁴ Each prophet will be ashamed of their vision by which they prophesy.
>> They won't put on a hairy robe*ᶜ* in order to deceive.
>>
>> ⁵ Each one will say, 'I am not a prophet! I am a farmhand,*ᵈ* for someone
>> sold me *as a slave* when I was young.'
>>
>> ⁶ Then someone will reply, 'What are these wounds between your arms?'
>> He will answer, 'They are the wounds I was given*ᵉ* in the house of
>> my friends.'

---

a   Since Shemei was a common name in Levite clans, this reference is unclear.
b   Literally, "father and mother who gave birth to him"; twice in this verse.
c   "Hairy robe": the sign of a prophet (see 2 Kings 1:8; Matthew 3:4).
d   Literally, "a worker of the ground."
e   Literally, "Those with which I was wounded."

The Purification of Israel

⁷ "Awake, O sword, against my shepherd and against the man associated with me, declares the Lord of Armies. Strike the shepherd, and the sheep will be scattered, and I will turn my hand against the little ones. ⁸ In the whole land, declares the Lord, two-thirds will be cut down and perish, but one-third will remain in it. ⁹ I will take the third through the fire and refine them like silver is refined. I will test them like gold is tested. They will call on my name, and I will answer them. I will say, 'They are my people,' and they will say, 'The Lord is my God.'"

14 Zechariah

¹ Listen! The day of the Lord is coming when the spoil *taken from* you, *Jerusalem,* will be divided up among you. ² I will gather all the nations to Jerusalem for war. The city will be captured, the houses plundered, and the women raped. Half of the city will go into exile, but the remainder of the people won't be cut off from the city.

³ Then the Lord will go out and fight against those nations, as he fights on a day of battle.

⁴ His feet will stand that day on the Mount of Olives, which is before Jerusalem to the east. The Mount of Olives will be split in half from east to west, *forming* a huge valley. Half of the mountain will be removed to the north and half to the south.

⁵ You will flee by my mountain valley, for the valley of the mountains will reach to Azel. You will flee like you fled from the earthquake in the days of Uzziah king of Judah. ⁶ On that day there will be no light, cold, or frost.^a

Then the Lord my God will come with all the holy ones with him.
⁷ It will be a unique day, known to the Lord, neither day nor night. But at evening time there will be light.

⁸ On that day^b
living waters will flow out of Jerusalem,
half of them *will flow* to the eastern sea and half of them to the western sea—in summer as well as in winter.
⁹ The Lord will be king over all the earth.

The Lord will be the only *god worshiped.*
His name will be the only *name.*

---

a   Or "there will be no light; the glorious ones will congeal." The Hebrew is uncertain.
b   "On that day" repeats in verse 9 and the start of verse 20.

¹⁰ The whole land, from Geba to Rimmon south of Jerusalem, will be changed to be like the *southern* Arabah.ᵃ But Jerusalem will be raised up and remain on its site from the Benjamin Gate to the place of the First Gate, to the Corner Gate, and from the Tower of Hananel to the royal winepresses.

¹¹ People will live in Jerusalem, and the curse will be no more.
Jerusalem will live securely.

> ¹² This will be the plague with which the LORD will strike all the peoples who make war on Jerusalem:

>> Their flesh will rot while they are standing on their feet, their eyes will rot in their sockets, and their tongues will rot in their mouths. ¹³ On that day a great panic from the LORD will fall on them. They will grab each other's hands and attack each other.ᵇ ¹⁵ So also will be the plague on the horse, the mule, the camel, the donkey, and all the livestock that will be in those camps.

¹⁴ Judah also will fight at Jerusalem. The wealth of all the surrounding nations will be gathered: gold, silver, and *costly* clothing in huge quantities.

¹⁶ All who survive from all the nations who attack Jerusalem will go up from year to year to worship the King, the LORD of Armies, and to celebrate the Festival of Shelters.

> ¹⁷ Any of the families of the earth that do not go up to Jerusalem to worship the King, the LORD of Armies, will have no rain *fall* on them.

>> ¹⁸ If the family of Egypt does not go up nor enter, no *rain will fall* on them. This is the plague with which the LORD will strike the nations who do not go up to celebrate the Festival of Shelters.

>>> ¹⁹ This will be the punishment of Egypt and the punishment of all the nations who do not go up to celebrate the Festival of Shelters.

²⁰ There will be *inscribed* on the bells of the horses, "Holy to the LORD."
The cooking pots in the temple will be like the bowls before the altar.

²¹ Every cooking pot in Jerusalem and Judah will be holy to the LORD of Armies. Everyone who brings a sacrifice will take some of the pots and cook in them. There will no longer be a Canaanite in the temple of the LORD of Armies on that day.

---

a "*Southern* Arabah": a desolate, hot, and dry area with little rain that includes the Dead Sea and runs south to Aqaba.

b Literally, "And the hand of one will be lifted against the hand of his neighbor."

Malachi

1 *Malachi*

¹ A prophecy: the word of the Lord to Israel through Malachi.

Admonition to Unfaithful Priests

² The Lord says:
"I have loved you,
but you say,
'How have you loved us?'
Here's how:
Wasn't Esau Jacob's brother?*ᵃ* declares the Lord.
But
I loved *your ancestor* Jacob, ³ and
I hated Esau.
I made his mountains a desolation and his inheritance *a place* for the
jackals in the wilderness.
⁴ Although Edom*ᵇ* says,
'We are beaten down, but we will return and rebuild our ruins,'
the Lord of Armies says this:
They may build, but I will tear down.
They will be called the Wicked Territory, the people with whom the Lord
is angry forever.
⁵ Your eyes will see it, and you will say, 'The Lord is great beyond the
territory of Israel.'

⁶ "A son honors his father and a slave his master.
So if I have been a father *to you,*
where is my honor?
And if I have been your master,
where is my respect? says the Lord of hosts to you,
O priests who despise my name.
But you say,
'How have we despised your name?'
⁷ *I say*
you are presenting defiled food on my altar.
But you say,
'How have we defiled you?'
Here's how:
It is
when you say of the table of the Lord, 'It is despised,' ⁸ and
when you bring forward a blind *animal* for sacrifice.

---

a   See Genesis 25:25–26.
b   "Edom": the land of Esau's descendants.

Is it not evil
    when you bring forward lame or diseased *animals*?
Is it not wrong?
        Try offering them to your governor.
            Would he be pleased with you?
            Would he accept you with favor?*ᵃ* says the Lᴏʀᴅ of Armies.

⁹ "The Lᴏʀᴅ of Armies says,
    Now, present a petition*ᵇ* before God that he may be gracious. With *an offering*
    like this from your hands, do you expect him to accept*ᶜ* any of you with favor?

¹⁰ "If only someone among you would shut the gates
        so that no one would light useless fires on my altar!
    I am not pleased with you, says the Lᴏʀᴅ of Armies, and
    I will accept no offering from your hands.
        ¹¹ For from where the sun rises to where it sets,
            my name will be great among the nations.
        In every place
            incense will be offered in my name, and
            a pure grain offering *will be brought to me*; for
            my name will be great among the nations, says the Lᴏʀᴅ of Armies.
¹² But as for you,
        you profane it when you say,
            'The table of the Lord is polluted and its food worthless'*ᵈ*—
            ¹³ and when you say,
            'What a nuisance!' and sniff disparagingly at it, says the Lᴏʀᴅ of Armies.
    And when you bring what is taken by robbery or a lame or diseased
    animal and offer that as sacrifices, *why* should I be pleased with what
    comes from your hands? says the Lᴏʀᴅ.
        ¹⁴ Cursed is the cheat who has a male in his flock and vows *to sacrifice* it but
        sacrifices something damaged to the Lord!
    "I am a great king, says the Lᴏʀᴅ of Armies, and my name is feared among
    the nations.

Malachi 2

¹ "And now, this commandment is for you, O priests.
    ² The Lᴏʀᴅ of Armies says,
        If you do not listen or take it to heart, to give my name glory,
        then
            I will send the curse upon you.
            I will curse your blessings.

---

a   Literally, "Would he lift up your head?"
b   Literally, "soften the face of."
c   Literally, "will he accept."
d   Literally, "is defiled, and its fruit is contemptible food."

Indeed, I have cursed them *already,*
> because you are not taking it to heart. ³ Look!
I will rebuke your offspring .
I will rub the filth*ᵃ* of your festival *sacrifices* on your faces, and you will
be taken away with it.
> ⁴ Then you will know that I have sent this commandment to you so that my
> covenant with Levi will continue, says the Lᴏʀᴅ of Armies.

⁵ "My covenant was with Levi,*ᵇ*
> *a covenant of* life and peace.
I gave them to him for reverence,
> so he revered me and was in awe of my name.
> ⁶ Faithful instruction was in his mouth, and
> > iniquity was not found on his lips.
> He walked with me peacefully and uprightly, and
> he turned many away from iniquity.
> > ⁷ For the priest's lips should guard knowledge,
> > and *people* should seek instruction from his mouth.
For he is the messenger of the Lᴏʀᴅ of Armies.
⁸ "But
> you have turned aside from the way.
> You have made many stumble with your instruction.*ᶜ*
> You have corrupted the covenant of Levi, says the Lᴏʀᴅ of Armies.
⁹ So in turn I have made you despised and humiliated by all the people,
> because you are not keeping my ways and are showing partiality*ᵈ* with
> your instruction."*ᵉ*

Admonition to Unfaithful Judah

¹⁰ Don't all of us have one Father?
Didn't one God create us *all*?
Why then do we profane the covenant of our ancestors
> by committing treachery against each other?
¹¹ Judah has been treacherous.
An abominable thing has been done in Israel and Jerusalem:
> Judah has profaned the Lᴏʀᴅ's beloved sanctuary
> and married the daughter of a foreign god.
¹² May the Lᴏʀᴅ cut off from the tents of Jacob the one who does this, the tempter
and the responder,*ᶠ* even if they bring an offering to the Lᴏʀᴅ of Armies.*ᵍ*

---

a "Filth": a reference to the extremely smelly contents of the stomach of a cud-chewing animal such as a
   cow or goat.
b Literally, "with him."
c Or "in the law."
d Literally, "are lifting up faces."
e Or "partiality in *your interpretation of* the law.
f Literally, "he who awakens and he who answers."
g The Hebrew is uncertain.

¹³ This is another thing you do:

> You cover the Lord's altar with tears,
>> weeping and moaning, because he no longer looks with favor on your offerings or accepts them with pleasure from your hands.

¹⁴ Yet you say, "Why?"

I say,

> Because the Lord is a witness between you and the wife of your youth with whom you have been treacherous.
>> She is your companion, the wife *with whom* you are in a covenant. ¹⁵ Hasn't he made *them* one?ᵃ And body and spirit belong to him.

> What does the one *God* seek? Godly offspring.
>> So guard yourselves in your spirits *against marital unfaithfulness.* Do not break faith withᵇ the wife of your youth.
>> ¹⁶ For the Lord God of Israel says,
>>> "I hate divorce because it covers violence with one's garment,ᶜ says the Lord of Armies."

> So guard yourselves in your spirit,
>> and do not be unfaithful.

¹⁷ You have wearied the Lord with your words.

> But you say, "How have we wearied *him*?"

You weary him when you say,

> "Everyone who does evil is good in the eyes of the Lord, and he delights in them," or, "Where is the God of justice?"

Malachi 3

¹ *The Lord says,*

> "See! I am sending my messenger. He will clear the way before me. The Lord whom you seek will come suddenly to his temple, and watch! The messenger of the covenant in whom you delight will come, says the Lord of Armies."

² *And I wondered,*

> But
>> who can endure the day when he comes?
>> Who can stand when he appears?

> For
>> he will be like a refiner's fire, like a laundry soap.
>> ³ He will sit as a refiner and purifier of silver, and
>> he will purify the Levites and refine them like gold and silver.
>>> Then they will present righteous offerings to the Lord, ⁴ and the offerings of Judah and Jerusalem will be sweet to the Lord, like in days long ago, in former years.

---

a   See Genesis 2:24. The Hebrew of this sentence and the next one is unclear.

b   Or "betray" or "deceive."

c   Or "it covers one's garment with violence." In ancient eastern writings, a wife is sometimes referred to as a husband's garment. See Deuteronomy 22:30.

⁵ *And the Lord continued,*

"I will draw near to you for judgment.
I will witness against you speedily—against[a]
sorcerers,
adulterers,
those who swear falsely,
those who oppress wage laborers,
widows and orphans, and
those who turn aside the foreigner *seeking justice* and do not fear me, says the Lord of Armies.
⁶ For I, the Lord, do not change;
therefore you, descendants of Jacob, are not destroyed.
⁷ Since your ancestors' days, you have turned from my statutes and not kept *them.*

Call to Tithe

"The Lord of Armies says, 'Return to me, and I will return to you.'
"But you say,
'How will we return?'
⁸ *"I ask,*
'Can a mortal rob God? But you are robbing me.'
"But you reply,
'How are we robbing you?'
"And I tell you:
in tithes and offerings.
⁹ You are accursed,[b]
because the whole nation of you is robbing me!
¹⁰ Bring the entire tithe into the storehouse,
so there will be food in my temple.
Test me in this, says the Lord of Armies,
and see if I won't open the floodgates of heaven and pour out a blessing for you, more than you can contain.[c]
¹¹ I will keep pests[d] from destroying the produce of your fields.
The vines in the field won't drop their fruit before it ripens,[e]
says the Lord of Armies.
¹² All the nations will call you blessed,
for you will be *living in* a delightful land,
says the Lord of Armies.

---

a "Against" repeats before each of the next five practices.
b Literally, "You are cursed with a curse."
c Literally, "until wearing out enough."
d Literally, "I will rebuke the one that devours."
e Literally, "won't be bereaved for you."

The Faithful Few Favored over the Arrogant and Evildoers

[13] "Your words have been arrogant[a] toward me, says the Lord.

Yet you ask, 'What have we said against you?'
 [14] *This is what* you have said:
 'It is useless to serve God. What has been our reward for keeping
 his requirements and walking like *repentant* mourners before the
 Lord of Armies?'
 [15] *And you have complained,*
 'Now we call the arrogant "blessed." Not only are those who act
 wickedly built up, but even when they put God to the test, they escape.'"

[16] Then those who feared the Lord spoke among themselves,[b] and the Lord paid
attention and heard. A scroll of remembrance was written in his presence for
those who feared the Lord and esteemed his name.

[17] "They will be my Mine, says the Lord of Armies. I will make them my
treasured possession. I will have compassion on them, just like a parent
has compassion on their child who serves them. [18] You will again see *the
difference* between righteousness and wickedness, between one who serves
God and one who does not serve him.

Malachi **4**

[1] "For listen! The day is coming.
 It is burning like a furnace.
 All the arrogant and evildoers will be like stubble.
 The day that is coming will set them on fire, says the Lord of Armies.
 Neither root nor branch will be left to them.
 [2] But for you who fear my name,
 the sun of righteousness will rise up with healing in its wings.
 You will go out leaping about like calves *released* from the stall.
 [3] You will tread down the wicked,
 for they will be like ashes under the soles of your feet on the day I act,
 says the Lord of Armies.

[4] "Remember the law of my servant Moses,
 the statutes and judgments that I commanded to him on *Mount* Horeb before
 all Israel.

[5] "Look for it! I will send you Elijah the prophet before the day of the Lord comes—
the great and dreadful day. [6] He will turn the hearts of the parents to *their*
children and the hearts of the children to *their* parents; otherwise I will come and
strike the land with a curse."

---

a Literally, "You have strengthened your words against me."
b Literally, "spoke one to another."

Prophetic Books Glossary

Abomination	Something disgusting, horrible, shameful, and detestable.
Anoint	To pour or smear oil (commonly olive oil) upon someone. In religious life this is done as part of a religious ceremony upon a person's appointment to ministry (e.g., priesthood, pastoral) as a symbol of the divine transfer of powers and/or authority and/or responsibility. In ancient secular life, anointing was done for many reasons: to get relief from the sun, to promote healing, as part of infant care, to attend to one's appearance, or to honor a guest upon entering the house. The dead were anointed with perfume to help ameliorate the odor of decay.
Apostasy	To turn away from the Lord.
Arabah	Hebrew for "a desert, dry place." In Scripture the term refers to the depression that runs from the Sea of Galilee south to the Gulf of Aqaba. The Northern Arabah runs from the Sea of Galilee to the Dead Sea. The Southern Arabah runs from the Dead Sea to the Gulf of Aqaba. Since the formation of today's nation of Israel, the term refers to the area south of the Dead Sea at the Israel/Jordan border.
Aram	An area encompassing northern Canaan and today's Syria. Several independent city-states rose up within it. Because Damascus was the best known and most successful of these, it is sometimes referred to as Aram.
Aramaic	A Semitic language closely related to Hebrew. It became the language of region-wide communication by the eighth century BC, the time of King Hezekiah and the prophet Isaiah.
Are/is to	See "Shall."
Asherah	A Canaanite goddess, the mother of Baal. The Hebrew term is also used for the cult objects that were used in her worship: poles (similar to totem poles) and/or trees that were set up near altars.
Atonement	At-one-ment. When two persons, usually God and a human, come back into harmonious relationship because the one who offended the other has paid for any offense. Regarding sin against God, in the Old Testament, the payment was made through the sacrificial system. The priests "made atonement" by offering to God the sacrifices brought by the Israelites.
Baal	The Canaanite storm God and the male god of fertility. In Canaanite mythology, Baal had intercourse every year with Ashtaroth, the goddess of fertility, which made the crops grow. Each region had its own god (e.g., Baal of Peor, meaning the one worshiped on Mount Peor).
Blaspheme	To slander or defame a person by falsehood. To blaspheme God is similar, although the consequences are infinitely more serious. It includes many kinds of acts, from cursing God to slighting God (i.e., taking him lightly, as of little account).

Bless, blessed	God toward people: to watch over, protect, bestow spiritual prosperity (holiness) or material prosperity (e.g., "God will bless us.").
	People toward God: to declare approval and support. To praise and/or honor and worship as good (e.g., "I will bless the Lord.").
	People toward people: to provide a benefit or meet a person's need or to call upon God for his care of someone (e.g., "May God bless you.").
Blessing	Verb: the act of asking God to bless.
	Noun: the spiritual or material prosperity or happiness resulting from being blessed.
Bowed down	A range of actions that all include bending the knee(s) and bowing the head by an inferior person toward their superior. It was the normal gesture by which one acknowledged the lordship of the person before them.
Bread	The Hebrew word for "bread," *lechem*, may also mean "food."
Burn, burn up	In the context of a sacrifice, "burn" has the meaning of offering something up to God. The verb could be rendered "offer up," "offer up in smoke," or "offer by fire."
Burnt offering	An offering to God, part of which was burned up. See "Sacrifice."
Call upon the name of the Lord	To invoke the name of the Lord in worship and/or prayer.
Canaan	Roughly, today's Lebanon, Israel, Palestinian territories, the western part of Jordan, and southwestern Syria. The exact borders are given in Numbers 34:3–12; however, some of the locations cited are uncertain.
Canaanite	"Canaanite" was used in a broad sense to include all the tribes living in the land west of the Jordan River that were occupied by Israel after their conquest. It was used in a narrower sense to refer to a specific tribe.
Chaldea	A part of Southern Babylonia. The term "Chaldeans" sometimes refers to residents of Babylonia led by Chaldean kings.
Circumcision	The cutting off of a male's foreskin. It is a sign of the Israelite's purification and commitment to a covenantal relationship with God. Under the Mosaic law, all male children were to be circumcised on the eighth day of their life. See Genesis 17:10–14 and Leviticus 12:3. It also means "circumcision of the heart" (removing the foreskin of the heart).
Citadel	A fortress guarding a city, typically on a high ground.
City	In the first two millennia BC, cities in Israel were seldom larger than five thousand people and typically much smaller. In *The Readable Bible*, "town" refers to communities of a hundred to a thousand families. "Village" refers to smaller communities; however, the population information is uncertain.
City gate	Where community leaders (elders, judges, etc.) sat in judgment and citizens gathered for public business, conversation, and fellowship. Because the city gate controlled who could enter or leave, and since it was where residents gathered and officials met the people, the term became a symbol for control of the city.
Clan	A number of families under a common leader and with a common ancestor. There may be several clans in a tribe.

Clean, unclean	These terms refer to whether a person, animal, or inanimate object fits God's conditions for use by his people in their daily lives or in his prescribed ceremonies. The terms do not necessarily refer to sinfulness or hygiene, although they sometimes do.
	Persons and objects became unclean primarily through contact with unclean persons or things. Animals were categorized as clean or unclean in the first five books of the Bible.
Consecrate	To set something apart for God or his service.
Covenant	A solemn agreement that binds the parties to one another in a permanent, defined relationship. It may define the obligations of a superior to an inferior and the reverse, or it may define the mutual obligations of equals.
	The term sometimes refers to the stone tablets with the Ten Commandments inscribed on them, and sometimes to the covenant relationship of God with Israel, under which they were to obey his laws and he was to be their provider and protector.
Cush	The region south of Egypt; today's Eritrea, Sudan, and Ethiopia.
Damascus	See "Aram."
Daughter of [location]	An expression meant to evoke a sense of pride and affection in the natives of that place, just as one should have toward their own daughter.
Defect	Any imperfection in a person or an animal. See also "Blemish."
Defile	To make dirty, corrupt, and/or ceremonially unclean (and therefore unfit for God's people or for use in God's work).
Desert	A dry, sandy region. See "Wilderness." Deserts may have wilderness areas.
Desolate	With regard to land, deserted and empty, without healthy vegetation. With regard to people, deserted by others and feeling dismal and/or empty.
Despise	Regard with contempt, loathe.
Detestable	See "Abomination."
Devote to the LORD	To set aside a physical object for God, to not use it for any personal purpose. It might be left alone or given to the temple.
to destruction	To destroy or kill, burn, or burn as a sacrifice.
Divination	Getting information by occult ritual (e.g., contact with supernatural spirits, reading so-called signs that indicate future events).
Drink offering	An offering made by pouring wine on the sanctuary floor.
Ephraim	A tribe of Israel named after the younger son of Joseph, adopted by Jacob. It became one of the largest tribes in Israel. Sometimes "Ephraim" is used as a metaphor for Northern Israel, and sometimes for the whole nation.
Eunuch	A castrated person, usually an official of the royal court.

Fast, fasting	A self-afflicting means of humbling yourself before God by refraining from nourishment for an extended period of time (in biblical times, at least from morning until evening). With prayer it is used as a visible sign of repentance, as a means to draw closer to God in times of special need (e.g., sickness, war, after great sin), and to prepare for receiving guidance from God. In Biblical times, those who fasted would often covered themselves with sackcloth and ashes. See "Sackcloth."
Fear	With reference to God, regard with deep reverence, respect, and awe.
Fell on his face/ before him/ to the ground	All three terms refer to lying facedown or kneeling before someone with one's hands on the ground, putting one's body in a reverential/yielded position as a gesture of submission and worship.
Festival	A period of "sacred assembly" for commemoration and/or celebration. Traditionally, festivals have been referred to as "feasts." Today "feast" is used primarily to refer to a large, elaborate meal, whereas "festival" includes much more than that, and may not include a meal at all. Thus, "festival" communicates the biblical concept more accurately. See "The Festivals of the Lord" table in the back of the book.
Firstfruits	The first and most highly valued part of the harvest. Metaphorically, it is the first of something which represents that there is more to come (e.g., Christ was the firstfruit of all believers—those who will be raised from the dead).
Flock	A group of goats or sheep.
Follow	In the context of rules and regulations, "follow," "keep," "observe," and "obey" all mean to adhere to, to abide by, or to act in accordance with.
Food	See "Bread."
Foreigner	Permanent non-Israelite residents among the Israelites, or travelers, or nomads who would appear periodically among the Israelites.
Freewill offering	A spontaneous offering of praise to the Lord—one not made for atonement or to fulfill a vow.
Glean	To gather the crop, usually grain, left behind by the harvesters.
Glory of God/of the Lord	The all-encompassing majesty of God (e.g., his lovingkindness, power, all-knowing presence, creativity, etc.) that man cannot fully comprehend. The display of God's presence and character seen in his creation and his acts and when he shows himself visibly (whether as light, fire, or whatever other form God chooses).
Hebrew	The term's origin is uncertain. Abraham and his descendants through Jacob are known as Hebrews.
Herd	A group of cattle or other large animals.
High priest	See "Priest."
Holy, become/ keep	Set apart for the purpose(s) or service of God. An object that is holy can be used only for God's purposes, usually in a ritual or sacrifice, or for consumption by the priests. Like a day that is holy, a person who is holy is one who has been set apart for God's purposes.

Holy Place	The area inside the tabernacle in front of the Most Holy Place. Lowercase, "a holy place" refers to the area inside the tabernacle curtains. God also occasionally designated other places as holy, such as the area around the burning bush in Exodus 3:5.
Horn	Metaphorically, a symbol of strength, power.
Horsemen	Cavalrymen and/or charioteers and/or those who took care of their horses.
Idol	A carved, cast metal, or pottery image believed to be a deity, or a cult object related to the worship of a God.
Inheritance	The land of Israel given to Abraham and his descendants as their inheritance (i.e., to be passed down). And God chose the Israelites as his inheritance (Psalms 28:9; 33:12).
Isaac	Abraham's second son; his only son by his wife Sarah.
Jacob	The original name for Isaac's second son (see Genesis 25:26). A metaphor for the Israelites (who are all descendants of Jacob, who was renamed "Israel" later in life).
Jubilee, Year of	Every fiftieth year, during which certain laws applied. See Leviticus 25:8–12.
Judah	The foremost tribe of Israel; the tribe of David, Solomon, and Jesus. It was named after its patriarch, the fourth son of Jacob. The name is often used as a metaphor for Israel. Upon the split of Israel into two kingdoms, its territory formed the bulk of the southern Kingdom of Judah.
Kerethites	The Kerethites and Pelethites were members of David's army who remained loyal to him in times of crisis, and may have formed his bodyguard. "While speculations about the two groups abound, the origin of them is unknown.
King	A king was the ruler over a city and its surrounding territory, which sometimes would have been a relatively small area. See "City."
Kir	An unknown place, believed by many to be the place from which Syrians originated.
Leaven	Any substance (usually yeast) added to dough to make it rise by releasing gas into it, thereby lightening and softening the dough. Since a very small amount affects a large amount of dough, the word is sometimes used as a metaphor for a small thing that has a large effect (such as sin). See Galatians 5:9. Under the Old Testament law, Jews were forbidden to eat or have leaven or leavened bread in the home on certain holy days. See "Unleavened."
Levites	The descendants of Levi (Jacob's third son). They served at the tabernacle. Aaron (Moses' brother) and his descendants were Levites; as priests they were a subset of the Levites. Only they could offer sacrifices. The Levites who were not descendants of Aaron helped the priests and took care of the tabernacle.
Locusts	Grasshoppers in their swarming phase.
Lord	The name of God is four Hebrew letters represented in English by *YHWH*. Out of reverence for God's name, we render the word as "Lord." The Hebrew, *YHWH*, cannot be translated exactly, but it is probably derived from the word "to be."

Lord God/ Lord my God/ Sovereign Lord	When "Yahweh" appears after *Adonai* (a Hebrew term of reverence for God), we usually render the two words as "Lord God." However, because these are synonymous terms next to each other, one reinforcing the other, they can equally well be rendered "Sovereign Lord." The Readable Bible rendering depends on the context.
Lord of Armies	Traditionally, "Lord of Hosts." While "hosts" refers to heavenly bodies, the Hebrew term rendered "hosts," *YHWH Tsabaoth*, literally is "armies." There is some debate as to whether "armies" should always be taken in a military sense or sometimes be taken in a general sense (e.g., "What an army of people.").
	The term speaks of God as the commander of the armies of both heaven and earth (even as the unseen power behind enemy armies) and the ruler of all spiritual beings. Since the Lord is over all forces in the spiritual, human, and natural realms, some English translations render *YHWH Tsabaoth* as "God Almighty." The Readable Bible uses "God Almighty" solely to translate the Hebrew term *El Shaddai*.
	Metaphorically, the term "hosts/armies" can be reflected back upon God, resulting in the term rendered "Sovereign Lord" in some Bibles.
Lord, my lord	Terms of respect used by a person of lower rank when addressing a person of higher rank.
Lovingkindness	Steadfast, faithful, loyal love; full of kindness and mercy. Hebrew: *chesed*.
Molech	A god worshiped in Canaan, sometimes by the sacrifice of children.
Most Holy Place	The area behind the veil inside the tabernacle, where God's presence dwelled over the ark of the covenant. Also known as the "Holy of Holies."
Mount Horeb	Another name for Mount Sinai.
Mount Sinai	The mountain where Moses received the Ten Commandments and other laws from God. It may or may not be where today's Mount Sinai is located, in Egypt at the southern end of the Sinai Peninsula.
Must	See "Shall."
Negev	A dry, mostly mountainous region ranging from the Mediterranean coast to the Dead Sea valley, from Hebron and Beersheba south to its apex at the north end of the Gulf of Aqaba. Though called a desert, it has areas of fertile soil with a foot of yearly rainfall (barely enough to grow a crop in a favorable year). The term can also denote "south."
New wine	Freshly pressed grape, unfermented.
Northern Israel	The Readable Bible text inserts "*Northern*" before "Israel" when the reference is clearly to the northern kingdom, that of the tribes north of the land of the tribe of Judah.
Obey	See "Follow."
Observe	See "Follow."
Offering	See "Sacrifice."
Oil	Usually from olives. Used as a healing, soothing substance and for cooking and anointing. See "Anoint."
Oracle	A message from a supernatural power given through another person.
Ordinances	See "Regulations."

Ox	A castrated bull. Castration makes bulls easier to control and, therefore, to use for labor such as pulling plows and carts.
Pagan	Follower of a polytheistic religion (i.e., one who believes in many gods).
Pagan nations	Nations other than Israel, usually those with many gods.
Passover	The annual celebration of Israel's departure from bondage in Egypt brought about by God killing all the firstborn of Egypt and passing over the firstborn of Israel. See Exodus 12 and Numbers 9.
Peace	Hebrew: *shalom*. A sense of wholeness, well-being free from disturbance.
Pharaoh	A title of the king of Egypt.
Philistine	The principal enemy of Israel, who occupied the coastal region (Philistia).
Priest	A mediator between God and his people, a spokesman for God. Jewish priests, descendants of Moses' brother Aaron, (a) taught the law, (b) handled the temple administration, and (c) received on behalf of God the sacrifices brought to the temple. See "Levites."
High priest a.k.a. chief priest	Literally, "the anointed priest." As the highest-ranking priest, he had special garments (see Exodus 28:1–43; 39:2–31) and, among other special duties, on the annual Day of Atonement he was the only priest allowed to enter the Most Holy Place to atone for the guilt of the sins of Israel. Sometimes the office was shared. A retired chief priest was also addressed as and referred to as a chief priest. When the Greek term is referring to more than one high priest (i.e., the current high priest plus former high priests), The Readable Bible renders "chief priests."
Prince	A tribal ruler or leader, not necessarily the son of a king.
Profane (verb)	To show disrespect or to make a person or thing ritually unclean.
Prophecy	That which has been spoken on God's behalf. Sometimes an act of prophecy involves the foretelling of something that will occur in the future.
Prophesy	To speak on God's behalf.
Prophet	A spokesperson for God whose primary task was to set before people the truths and expectations of God. Occasionally, some prophets also foretold events, but this was a small part of their ministry.
Redeem	To pay a specified amount to be released from an obligation, to be delivered from a controlling power, or to recover ownership of something that was given to, claimed by, or dedicated to God.
Regard	To think of a person in a special way.
Regulations	Regulations, rules, and stipulations are terms for actions that are either required or forbidden by God. Common terms in English translations include decrees, judgments, laws, ordinances, rules, regulations, stipulations, and statutes. The terms are basically synonymous.

Righteous/ righteousness	In secular life, to be righteous is to act with integrity with regard to what is right, to have high moral and ethical standards. In the Bible, righteousness is the state of being that God intends for people. A righteous person is one whose life is in conformity with the inner character and standards of God. One who is righteous acts in accordance with God's law as written in the Bible and written upon the heart of the believer. The Bible teaches that God makes righteous those who follow him (i.e., who put their faith in Jesus Christ as their Lord and Savior).
Rules	See "Regulations."
Sackcloth	Very rough cloth used primarily for grain sacks. It was also made into crude, coarse clothing that was worn to afflict the wearer and show others they were mourning on account of the loss of a loved one or other tragedy, or to show they were in a state of repentance on account of sin. Oftentimes mourners also threw ashes upon themselves (hence the familiar phrase "sackcloth and ashes").
Sacred	Set apart for the purpose(s) and/or service of God. See "Holy."
Sacrifice	In the Old Testament, and until the destruction of the temple in Jerusalem in AD 70, a gift/offering to God, often presented to him by burning it. It was offered to express appreciation for what God had done for the offerer or to appease God for the offerer's sin (see Leviticus 1–7). The owner made the offering as an act of faith, believing that the Lord will accept it as an outward sign of their inward belief in him, their acceptance of his lordship, and their desire to be in a harmonious relationship with him.
Samaria/ Samaritan	A people similar to Jews who lived in the region of Samaria (roughly, the area between the Mediterranean Sea and the Jordan River north of Jericho up to Mount Carmel). Samaritans are partially descended from the same ancestors as the Jews. The Samaritan religion has similarities to Judaism. Its followers claim the first five books of the Jewish Scriptures as their own. However, they consider Mount Gerizim (where they had temple worship rather than in Jerusalem) the holiest place. In Jesus' time, Jews looked down upon Samaritans and avoided their territory and speaking to them. Jews did not eat with, drink with, or touch Samaritans for fear of becoming ceremonially unclean.
Sanctify	To make holy, morally pure. See "Holy" and "Consecrate."
Sanctuary	In the Old Testament, the place where God dwells, which was set aside for God's service. Sometimes it refers to the Most Holy Place within the tabernacle/temple and sometimes to the whole area within the temple courtyard border. See "Temple."
Seir	The country around the Seir Highlands, southeast of the Dead Sea.
Selah	The meaning of this Hebrew term is uncertain. It is generally believed to be a musical notation (e.g., interlude, repeat). Since its meaning is uncertain and it adds nothing meaningful to Scripture, we present it in light text at the right-side margin.

Septuagint	A Greek translation of the Old Testament written in the third and second centuries BC. The translation philosophy and quality varies by section. Its Pentateuch is quite literal and accurate. The Historical Books and Prophets are a more relaxed translation, and the Wisdom Literature and Poetical Books have some very loosely translated parts. Nevertheless, it was the Bible used in New Testament times. Almost every New Testament quotation of the Old Testament is from it.
Shall	"Shall," "is/are to," and "must" are used to indicate a command or to emphatically state a fact (e.g., "The Lord shall reign forever"). "Will" is used to point to a future event or condition.
Shekel	A measure of weight and value. About 0.37 troy ounces (11.5 grams), about the weight of two American nickels or two twenty-cent euro coins.
Sheol	The place of the dead. Sometimes refers to a person's grave or to death in general.
Shiloh	An important city about twenty miles north-northeast of Jerusalem that was a prominent center of worship in the time of the judges. It lost its significance soon afterward. The ark of the covenant resided there during the time of the judges and throughout Samuel's lifetime.
Sojourn	To reside temporarily, live as a foreigner. See "Foreigner."
Sons of man/men	A metaphor for mankind.
Soul	The Hebrew term translated as "soul," *nephesh,* may also be rendered as a personal pronoun. For example, "*nephesh* sings" can be rendered "my soul sings" or "I sing."
Statutes	See "Regulations."
Stiff-necked	Stubborn, haughty in one's obstinacy. Derived from the picture of a beast of burden refusing to be directed by its master.
Swear	Solemnly promise; promise with an oath.
Thummim	See "Urim and Thummim."
Tarshish	Mentioned in Scripture as a major trading place with a fleet of ships and as a source of minerals. Whether Tarshish is a trading destination and/or a city or place is unknown. Tarshish is probably in modern-day Spain or perhaps Tunisia. The designation "ships of Tarshish" meant well-built vessels that could be sailed over journeys of hundreds of miles in open water, rather than smaller, commuter vessels that stayed within sight of land.
Tithe	One-tenth of what is produced or earned. Given by the Israelites as an offering to God.
Town	See "City."
Transgression	Failure to fulfill a command, law, or duty.
Tribe	One of the twelve tribes of Israel (Reuben, Simeon, Judah, Dan, Naphtali, Gad, Asher, Issachar, Zebulun, Benjamin, Ephraim, and Manasseh), descendants of eleven of Jacob's twelve sons. Rather than possess land and farm, Levi's sons served as priests, tabernacle attendants, and teachers. Joseph's sons Ephraim and Manasseh were each established as a full tribe to complete the number twelve (see Genesis 48:5).

Unclean	See "Clean, unclean."
Unleavened	Made without yeast or any other leavening agent. Unleavened bread is flat, tough, and chewy or crisp. It was a sign of poverty and/or temporariness. See "Leaven."
Wadi	A water-worn depression that is usually dry.
Wilderness	An uninhabited area with desertlike characteristics, though not necessarily sandy. It is sometimes mountainous, often with terraces and steep cliffs from highlands to ravines more than a thousand feet below.
Winnow	To toss crushed grain kernels in the air, so the bits of dirt and husk will be separated from the heavier, edible parts.
Wormwood	An herb (*Artemisia absinthium*) that produces an extraordinarily bitter-tasting oil. Sometimes it is used as a metaphor for bitterness.
Yahweh	See "LORD."
Yearling	An animal that is between one and two years old.
Zion	At first, a Jebusite city on a high point, Mount Zion. After David captured the city, Jerusalem was built upon it. Zion is sometimes a metaphor for Jerusalem and sometimes a metaphor for Israel.

FAMILIAR VERSES

Familiar Verses in Hosea

4:6a	My people are destroyed for lack of knowledge.
6:6	For I delight in loyal love, not sacrifice, and in the knowledge of God rather than burnt offerings.
8:7a	For they'll sow the wind and reap the whirlwind.
11:9b	I am the Holy One in your midst; I won't come in wrath.

Familiar Verses in Joel

2:28	After this, I will pour out my Spirit on all people; your sons and daughters will prophesy. Your elders will dream dreams, and your young men will see visions.
2:31–32a	[31] The sun will be turned into darkness and the moon into blood before the coming of the great and awesome day of the LORD. [32a] All who call on the name of the LORD will be saved.
3:10	Beat your plowshares into swords and your pruning hooks into spears. Let the weakling say, "I am strong!"

Familiar Verses in Amos

3:7	For the Lord GOD does nothing without revealing his plan to his servants the prophets.
4:12c	Prepare to meet your God, O Israel!
5:24	Let justice roll on like waters and righteousness like a never-failing stream.
7:14	Amos answered Amaziah: "I am neither a prophet nor the son of a prophet. I am a shepherd and a tender of sycamore fig trees."

Familiar Verses in Jonah

1:17	The LORD appointed a huge fish to swallow Jonah, and he was in the fish's belly for three days and three nights.
2:4b	I will again look toward your holy temple.

Familiar Verses in Micah

4:3b	They will beat their swords into plowshares and their spears into pruning hooks.
5:2a	But as for you, Bethlehem of Ephrathah, though you are small among the clans of Judah, one who will be the ruler of Israel for me will come out of you.
6:8	He has told you, O mortal, what is good. What does the LORD require from you? But to act justly, to love mercy, and to walk humbly with your God.

Familiar Verses in Nahum

1:7a	The LORD is good, a fortress in a time of distress; he knows those who take refuge in him.

Familiar Verses in Habakkuk

2:4b	The righteous one will live by faith.
3:2b	I am in awe of your work, O LORD. Bring it to life in our time; make it known in our years. In wrath remember mercy.
3:19a	GOD, the Lord, is my strength. He makes my feet like the feet of a deer, and he leads me onto the heights.

Familiar Verses in Zephaniah

| 3:17 | The LORD your God is among you, a warrior who saves; he will rejoice over you with joy; he will quiet you with his love; he will rejoice over you with songs of joy. |

Familiar Verses in Zechariah

1:3	Therefore tell the people, the LORD of Armies says this: "Return to me, declares the LORD of Armies, and I will return to you." The LORD of Armies has spoken.
3:2	The LORD said to the Accuser, "The LORD rebuke you, Satan! The LORD, who has chosen Jerusalem, rebuke you! Isn't this man a burning stick snatched from the fire?"
4:6	He replied, "This is the word of the LORD to Zerubbabel: 'Not by might nor by power but by my Spirit, says the LORD of Armies.'"
4:10a	For who despised the day of small things?
9:9	Shout with abounding joy, Daughter Zion! Cry aloud, Daughter Jerusalem! Look! Your king is coming to you. He is righteous and victorious, humble and riding on a donkey, on a colt, the foal of a donkey.
11:12–13	[12] I said to them, "If it is good in your opinion, give me my wages; if not, keep it." So they weighed out thirty pieces of silver for my wages. [13] The LORD said to me, "Throw it to the potter"—that magnificent price at which I was valued by them! So I took the thirty pieces of silver and threw them to the potter at the temple.

Familiar Verses in Malachi

1:8	[It is] when you bring forward a blind animal for sacrifice. Is it not evil when you bring forward lame or diseased animals? Is it not wrong? Try offering them to your governor. Would he be pleased with you? Would he accept you with favor? says the LORD of Armies.
1:10–11a	[10] If only someone among you would shut the gates so that no one would light useless fires on my altar! I am not pleased with you, says the LORD of Armies, and I will accept no offering from your hands. [11a] For from where the sun rises to where it sets, my name will be great among the nations.
1:14	Cursed is the cheat who has a male in his flock and vows to sacrifice it but sacrifices something damaged to the Lord! "I am a great king, says the LORD of Armies, and my name is feared among the nations."
2:6	Faithful instruction was in his mouth, and iniquity was not found on his lips. He walked with me peacefully and uprightly, and he turned many away from iniquity.

2:15–16a	[15] Hasn't he made them one? And body and spirit belong to him. What does the one God seek? Godly offspring. So guard yourselves in your spirits against marital unfaithfulness. Do not break faith with the wife of your youth. [16a] For the LORD God of Israel says, "I hate divorce."
3:1	The Lord says, "See! I am sending my messenger. He will clear the way before me. The Lord whom you seek will come suddenly to his temple, and watch! The messenger of the covenant in whom you delight will come, says the LORD of Armies."
3:6a, 7b	[6a] I, the LORD, do not change. [7b] Return to me, and I will return to you.
3:8–12	[8] I ask, "Can a mortal rob God? But you are robbing me." But you reply, "How are we robbing you?" And I tell you: "In tithes and offerings. [9] You are accursed, because the whole nation of you is robbing me! [10] Bring the entire tithe into the storehouse, so there will be food in my temple. Test me in this, says the LORD of Armies, and see if I won't open the floodgates of heaven and pour out a blessing for you, more than you can contain. [11] I will keep pests from destroying the produce of your fields. The vines in the field will not drop their fruit before it ripens, says the LORD of Armies. [12] All the nations will call you blessed, for you will be living in a delightful land, says the LORD of Armies."
3:16	Then those who feared the LORD spoke among themselves, and the LORD paid attention and heard. A scroll of remembrance was written in his presence for those who feared the LORD and esteemed his name.
4:5–6a	[5] Look for it! I will send you Elijah the prophet before the day of the LORD comes—the great and dreadful day. [6a] He will turn the hearts of the parents to their children and the hearts of the children to their parents.

Note on Dates of Events

The exact year in which any event in the Bible took place is speculative. Today's *anno Domini* dating system was not invented until about AD 1525, more than a thousand years after the last words of Scripture were written. Before adopting the *anno Domini* system, people kept track of years by the regnal system, tying events to the year of the reigning king, governor, or lesser official (e.g., "in the fifteenth year of Tiberias Caesar"). People simply were not concerned about exact dates.

Because the biblical records were not written with the idea of recording dates, the information is incomplete. While there are means of estimating the dates, they are all guesstimates. The dates we present fall within the generally accepted date ranges used by biblical scholars.

PEOPLE LIST[a]

People in Hosea

Name	Key Facts	Events	Chapter
David	King of Israel	Mentioned	3
Gomer	Daughter of Diblaim, a prostitute Wife of Hosea	Married Hosea and had children	1
Hosea	Son of Beeri Author of book Prophet	Told to marry a prostitute and have children Told to love his adulterous wife	1 3
Jacob	Patriarch of Israel Ancestor of the Jewish people Younger twin of Esau	Mentioned	12
Jezreel, a.k.a. God Sows	Hosea and Gomer's first son	Mentioned	1
Lo-Ammi a.k.a. Not My People	Gomer's second son, born while she was married to Hosea but not Hosea's	Mentioned	1
Lo-Ruhamah a.k.a. Not Loved	Gomer's daughter, born while she was married to Hosea but not Hosea's	Mentioned	1

People in Amos

Name	Key Facts	Events	Chapter
Amaziah	Priest at Bethel False prophet	Accused Amos of conspiracy Amos prophesied his exile, death, and family's destruction.	7
Amos	Shepherd from Tekoa Author of book	Called to prophesy against Israel Saw numerous visions of Israel's exile and destruction	1 1–9
Jeroboam	King of Israel	Mentioned	1, 7
Uzziah	King of Judah	Mentioned	1

---

a Joel, Obadiah, Nahum, Habakkuk, and Zephaniah are not listed, as those books do not mention anyone by name.

People in Jonah

Name	Key Facts	Events	Chapter
Captain of ship		Pleaded with Jonah to pray they don't perish	1
Jonah	Son of Amittai Author of book Prophet	Boarded ship to escape God's call Swallowed by a fish Prayed, then fish spit him out Called Nineveh to repent Wallowed in self-pity after city is spared	1 2 3 4
King of Nineveh		Called for a fast and mourning as signs of repentance	3

People in Micah

Name	Key Facts	Events	Chapter
Aaron	Moses' brother, first high priest	Mentioned	6
Abraham	Patriarch of Israel	Mentioned	7
Ahab	Wicked king of Israel	Mentioned	6
Ahaz, a.k.a. Jehoahaz	King of Judah	Mentioned	1
Balaam	Son of Beor, evil prophet	Mentioned	6
Balak	King of Moab	Mentioned	6
Hezekiah	King of Judah	Mentioned	1
Jacob	Patriarch of Israel	Mentioned	7
Jotham	King of Judah	Mentioned	1
Micah	Prophet from Moresheth Author of book	Prophesied judgment and restoration for Israel	1–7
Miriam	Moses' sister	Mentioned	6
Moses	Prophet who led Israel out of Egypt and in the wilderness	Mentioned	6
Omri	Wicked king of Israel, father of Ahab	Mentioned	6

People in Haggai

Name	Key Facts	Events	Chapter
Darius	King of Persia	Mentioned	1
Haggai	Prophet Author of book	Prophesied to returning exiles concerning the rebuilding of the temple	1–2
Joshua	Son of Jehozadak, high priest	Called by God to rebuild the temple Encouraged to be strong in the face of opposition	1 2
Zerubbabel	Son of Shealtiel, governor of Judah Descendant of King David	Called by God to rebuild the temple Encouraged to be strong in the face of opposition Told he is chosen by God	1 2

People in Zechariah

Name	Key Facts	Events	Chapter
Darius	King of Persia	Mentioned	1
David	King of Israel	Mentioned	12–13
Heldai	One of the exiles	Gave an offering Promised a crown as a memorial in the Lord's temple	6
Jedaiah	One of the exiles	Gave an offering Promised a crown as a memorial in the Lord's temple	6
Joshua	Son of Jehozadak, high priest	Received fine robes instead of filthy robes in Zechariah's vision Told to walk in God's ways Crowned by Zechariah as a symbol of the one to come who will rebuild the temple	3 6
Josiah a.k.a. Hen	Son of Zephaniah	Received Zechariah and other exiles at his house Promised a crown as a memorial in the Lord's temple	6
Levi	Father of the Levites, those called by God to serve in the temple	Mentioned	12
Nathan	Prophet of Israel	Mentioned	12
Regem-Melech	Representative from Bethel	Sent to make a petition to the Lord	7

Sharezer	Representative from Bethel	Sent to make a petition to the Lord	7
Tobijah	One of the exiles	Gave an offering Promised a crown as a memorial in the Lord's temple	6
Zechariah	Son of Berekiah, prophet and priest Author of book	Saw visions of Israel's future blessing, forgiveness, and restoration Prophesied judgment against evil in Israel and among the nations	1–14
Zerubbabel	Son of Shealtiel, governor of Judah	Chosen by God to rebuild the temple Encouraged to be strong in the face of opposition	4

People in Malachi

Name	Key Facts	Events	Chapter
Elijah	Prophet of Israel	Mentioned	4
Esau	Older twin of Jacob	Mentioned	1
Jacob	Patriarch of Israel	Mentioned	1
Malachi	Prophet Author of book	Rebuked Israel's unfaithfulness to God Called Israel to repentance and warned them about the day of the Lord	1–4
Moses	Prophet who led Israel out of Egypt and in the wilderness	Mentioned	4

Subject Index

The subject begins at the cited verse.

Adultery	Hos. 2:2; 3:1; 4:2; 7:4; Mal. 3:5
Angels	Zech. 1:9,19; 2:3; 3:3; 4:1; 5:2; 12:8
Branch, the	Zech. 3:8; 6:12
Covenant, new	Hos. 2:18; Zech. 9:11
Day of the Lord	Joel 1:15; 2:1,11,31; Amos 5:18; Obad. 1:15; Zeph. 1:7,14; Zech. 14:1; Mal. 4:1,5
Divorce	Mal. 2:16
Fasting	Joel 1:14; 2:12; Jon. 3:5; Zech. 7:5; 8:19
Fish	Jon. 1:17; 2:1,10
God	
Anger of	Hos. 5:10; 12:14; 13:11; Jon. 3:9; Mic. 7:9; Nah. 1:2, 6; Hab. 3:12; Zeph. 1:18; 2:2; 3:8; Zech. 1:2,15; 7:12; 8:2
Blessings of	Joel 2:14,19; Zech. 10:1; Mal. 3:10
Compassion of	Hos. 2:19, 23; 11:8; Zech. 1:16; 10:6; Mal. 3:17
Creator	Amos 4:13; 5:8; 9:5; Jon. 1:9; Hab. 3:9; Zech. 10:1; 12:1; Mal. 2:10
Defends Israel	Zeph. 3:17; Hag. 2:4; Zech. 9:15; 10:5; 12:4; 14:3
Desires loyal love	Hos. 6:6; 10:12; 12:6; Mic. 6:8; 7:18; Zech. 7:9
Everlasting	Hab. 1:12; 3:6
Faithful	Hos. 2:19; Hag. 2:5
Fear of	Hos. 10:3; Jon. 1:9; Mic. 6:9; Mal. 1:14; 3:5,16; 4:2
Gracious	Jon. 4:2
Heals	Hos. 6:1; 7:1; 11:3; 14:4; Mal. 4:2
Husband to Israel	Hos. 2:7,16
Jealous	Nah. 1:2; Zeph. 1:18; 3:8; Zech. 1:13; 8:2
Judgment of, for	Hos. 5:1; 6:5; 10:4; 12:2,14; Joel 3:2,12; Zeph. 1:12; Hag. 2:21; Mal. 3:5
Ammon	Amos 1:13
Assyria	Zeph. 2:13
Cush	Zeph. 2:12
Damascus	Amos 1:3; Zech. 9:1
Edom	Amos 1:11; Obad. 1:1
Egypt	Joel 3:19
Gaza	Amos 1:6; Zeph. 2:4; Zech. 9:5
Israel	Amos 2:6; 8:2
Judah	Amos 2:4; Zeph. 1:4
Moab	Amos 2:1; Zeph. 2:9
Nineveh	Jon. 3:4; Nah. 1:8; 2:1
Philistia	Joel 3:4; Zeph. 2:5; Zech. 9:6
Tyre	Joel 3:4; Amos 1:9; Zech. 9:2
Just	Hos. 2:19; Mic. 7:9; Zeph. 3:5
Longs to forgive	Jon. 3:10; Mic. 7:18

Love of	Hos. 11:1; Joel 2:13; Jon. 2:8; 4:2; Zeph. 3:17; Mal. 1:2
Mercy of	Joel 2:13; Jon. 4:2, 11; Mic. 7:19
Power of	Jon. 1:4; Nah. 1:3; Hab. 3:4; Hag. 2:21
Provider	Hos. 2:8; 12:5; 14:8; Joel 2:19
Pure	Hab. 1:13; Zeph. 3:5
Refuge, a	Joel 3:16; Nah. 1:7; Zeph. 3:12
Rescues	Joel 2:20; Jon. 2:6; Mic. 4:10; 5:6; Hab. 3:13; Zeph. 3:19; Zech. 8:13; 9:15
Restores the captives	Hos. 6:11; Joel 3:1; Amos 9:14; Mic. 5:6; Zeph. 3:20; Zech. 10:6
Righteous	Hos. 2:19; Mic. 7:9; Zeph. 3:5
Salvation of	Jon. 2:9; Mic. 7:7; Hab. 3:8, 13, 18; Zeph. 3:17; Zech. 9:16; 10:6
Slow to anger	Joel 2:13; Jon. 4:2; Nah. 1:3
Spirit of	Joel 2:28; Mic. 2:7; 3:8; Hag. 2:5; Zech. 4:6; 6:8; 7:12
Temple of	Hos. 8:1; 9:5, 15; Joel 1:9, 14; 3:18; Jon. 2:4; Mic. 1:2; 3:12; 4:1; Hab. 2:20; Hag. 1:2, 7; 2:3, 15; Zech. 1:16; 4:9; 6:13; 8:9; 14:21; Mal. 3:1, 10
True, the	Hos. 12:4; 14:8; Joel 2:27
Vengeance of	Joel 3:21; Mic. 5:15; Nah. 1:2
Word of	Mic. 4:2; Mal. 4:4
God's people (Israel and Judah)	
Abandoned (forgot) God	Hos. 1:2; 2:13; 4:1, 10; 7:10; 8:14; 12:6; Zeph. 1:6
Adulterous	Hos. 2:2; 7:4
Called to repent	Hos. 2:2; 6:1; 10:12; 12:6; 14:1; Joel 2:12; Amos 5:4, 14; Mic. 6:8; Zeph. 2:3; Hag. 1:12; Zech. 1:3; 7:9; Mal. 3:7
Children of God	Hos. 1:10; 11:1, 10; 13:13; Mal. 1:6
Chosen ones	Amos 3:2; Zech. 13:9
Complacent	Amos 6:1
Covenant-Breakers	Hos. 8:1
Lack knowledge	Hos. 4:1, 6
Liars	Hos. 4:1; 7:13; 10:4, 13; 11:12; 12:1, 7; Amos 2:4; Mic. 6:12; Mal. 3:5
Loved by God	Hos. 2:19; 3:1; 11:1; 14:4
Prayers for them ignored	Mic. 3:4; Hab. 1:2; Zech. 7:13
Prostituted themselves	Hos. 1:2; 2:2, 12; 4:11; 5:3; 6:10; 9:1; Mic. 1:7
Proud	Hos. 5:5; 7:10; 12:6; Amos 6:8
Refused to return to God	Hos. 7:14; 11:5; Amos 4:8; Zeph. 3:1, 7; Hag. 2:17; Zech. 1:4; 7:11
Rejected by God	Hos. 4:6; 5:6; 9:15
Rejected God's law	Amos 2:4; Zeph. 1:6; 3:4; Zech. 7:12; Mal. 2:8
Remnant of	Amos 5:15; Mic. 2:12; 5:7; 7:18; Zeph. 2:7; 3:12; Hag. 1:12; 2:2; Zech. 8:6, 11
Restoration of	Hos. 1:10; 2:14; 3:5; 11:9; 12:9; 14:4; Joel 2:18, 25; 3:16; Amos 9:11; Obad. 1:17; Mic. 2:12; 4:8; 5:2; 7:15; Nah. 1:12; Hab. 3:16; Zeph. 3:9; Hag. 2:6; Zech. 1:16; 8:3, 11; 10:3; 12:2; 13:1; 14:1

Results of disobedience	
Barrenness	Hos. 9:12
Burning	Hos. 8:14; Joel 1:19; 2:3; Amos 2:5; 5:6
Death	Amos 2:14; 6:9
Desolation	Hos. 2:11; 5:9; Amos 7:9; Mic. 1:6; 7:13; Zeph. 3:6; Zech. 7:14
Destruction	Hos. 4:19; 5:14; 7:13; 8:1; 10:8, 14; Amos 3:11; 5:9; 9:1, 8; Mic. 2:3, 10; 3:12; 6:13; Hab. 1:3; Zeph. 1:13
Drought	Hos. 4:3; Amos 4:7; Hag. 1:11
Exile	Hos. 8:8; 9:3, 17; 10:5; 11:5; Amos 4:2; 5:27; 6:7; 7:17; Mic. 1:16; 4:10; Zech. 7:14
Famine	Hos. 2:3, 9; 7:16; 9:2; Joel 1:10; Amos 4:6; 8:11
Humiliation	Hos. 2:10
Mildew	Amos 4:9
Oppression	Amos 6:14
Plague	Amos 4:10
Poverty	Hos. 2:3, 9; 8:7; 13:15; Mic. 6:14; Hag. 1:6
Punishment	Hos. 1:4; 8:13; 9:7; Amos 3:2, 14; Zeph. 3:7
Shame	Hos. 4:9, 14; 10:6
Sorrow	Hos. 4:7, 19
Sword, the	Hos. 7:16; 11:6; 13:16; Amos 4:10; 7:9; 9:1; Mic. 6:14
Sacrifices not acceptable	Amos 5:21; Mic. 6:6; Mal. 1:7; 2:12
Shepherds of	Mic. 5:2; 7:14; Zech. 10:2; 11:16; 13:7
Sinned against God	Hos. 4:2, 7; 5:4; 6:7; 7:1, 13; 8:1, 11; 9:7, 15; 10:8; 12:8; 13:2, 12; Amos 2:6; 3:2, 14; 4:4; 5:12; 8:4; 9:8; Mic. 1:5; 2:1; 3:4, 8; 6:7, 16; 7:2; Zeph. 1:17; 3:1, 11; Mal. 2:10
Sought help from nations	Hos. 5:13; 7:11; 12:1
Stubborn	Hos. 4:16
Under a curse	Mal. 1:14; 2:2; 3:9
Worshiped idols	Hos. 2:8, 13; 3:1; 4:12; 5:11; 8:4, 13; 9:10; 10:1; 11:2; 13:1; Amos 5:5, 25; 8:14; Mic. 1:5, 13; Zeph. 1:5
Idols, worthlessness of	Hos. 8:6; Jon. 2:8; Hab. 2:18; Zech. 10:2
Jerusalem	
Holy	Joel 3:17; Obad. 1:17
New	Joel 3:17; Amos 9:11; Zech. 1:17; 2:4; 3:7; 8:3, 9, 15, 22; 12:2; 13:1; 14:1
Kings	Hos. 7:3; 8:4; 10:7; 13:11; Jon. 3:6; Mic. 2:13; 4:8; Nah. 3:18; Zech. 9:9; 14:9; Mal. 1:14
Latter days	Mic. 4:1
Locust plague	Joel 1:4; 2:25; Amos 7:1
Lord	See "God."
Prayer	Hos. 14:8; Jon. 1:14; 2:1; 4:2; Hab. 1:2; 3:1
Priests	Hos. 4:4; 5:1; 10:5; Joel 1:13; 2:17; Zeph. 1:4; 3:4; Hag. 2:11; Zech. 6:13; 7:3; Mal. 1:6; 2:1

Prophets	Hos. 4:5; 6:5; 9:7; 12:10; Joel 2:28; Amos 2:11; 3:7; Hag. 1:12; Zech. 1:4; 7:3; 8:9; Mal. 4:5
False	Amos 7:12; Mic. 2:11; 3:5, 11; Zeph. 3:4; Zech. 10:2; 13:2
Visions	
Clean garments	Zech. 3:1
Fire	Amos 7:4
Flying scroll	Zech. 5:1
Four chariots	Zech. 6:1
Four horns and craftsmen	Zech. 1:18
Gold lampstand	Zech. 4:2
Locusts	Amos 7:1
Lord, the	Amos 9:1
Measuring line	Zech. 2:1
Plumb line	Amos 7:7
Red horse	Zech. 1:8
Summer fruit	Amos 8:1
Two olive trees	Zech. 4:3, 11
Woman in a basket	Zech. 5:5
Prostitution	Hos. 1:2; 3:2; 4:11; 5:4; 6:10
Tithes	Amos 4:4; Mal. 3:8

Weights and Measures in Minor Prophets
Read about biblical weights and measures in "Translation Notes."

Capacity, dry	
Homer	6.3 bushels.
Lethek	3¼ bushels.
Coinage	
Shekel	About 0.4 avoirdupois ounce, about the weight of two American nickels or two twenty-cent euro coins.

The Jewish Calendar

Each month of the Jewish calendar begins upon a new moon, which year to year occurs on different days of our Gregorian calendar months and rarely on the first day of a month. Thus, the relationship of Jewish calendar months to our Gregorian calendar months varies year to year.

In addition to the Levitical festivals below, there are twelve new moon festivals, and every Sabbath is a day of complete rest.

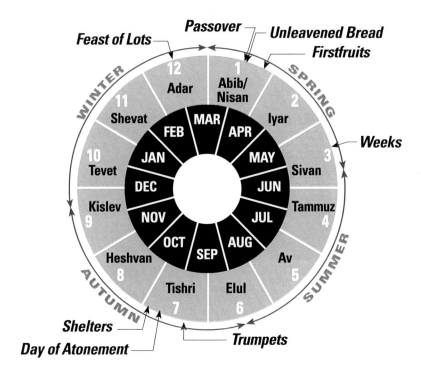

The Festivals of the Lord [a]

A sacred convocation is held on the first day of each festival. The offerings are in addition to the regular daily offerings, Sabbath offerings, and new moon offerings (see Numbers 28:3–15).

	Spring Festivals				Fall Festivals		
English Name	**Passover** [c]	**Unleavened Bread** [c]	**Firstfruits**	**Weeks** [c] (Pentecost, Harvest)	**Trumpets**	**Day of Atonement**	**Shelters** [c] (a.k.a. Tabernacles, Booths, Ingathering)
Hebrew Name	Pesach	Hag Hamatzot	Bikkurim	Shavuot	Rosh Hashanah	Yom Kippur	Sukkot
Purpose	Remember God passed over the Israelites when, to free them, he killed the firstborn of Egypt.	Remember leaving Egypt.	Recognize God's goodness in providing a crop.	Celebrate the grain harvest and God's giving of the Ten Commandments.	Celebrate the beginning of the new year.	Mourn sin, afflict the soul, and seek atonement.	Remember the exodus and forty years of wandering.
Dates [b] **Hebrew**	Abib 14	Abib 15–21	Abib 16	50th day after Passover	Tishri 1	Tishri 10	Tishri 15
Gregorian		Late March to late April		Mid-May to mid-June		Mid-September to mid-October	
Number of Days	One day	Six or seven days	One day	One day	One day	One day	Seven days
Offerings and Practices	Burnt and sin offerings. Seder meal. Eat no leavened bread. Rest, no work.	Daily offerings by fire. Eat no leavened bread. Rest, no work on 1st and 7th days.	Wave offering of sheaf of firstfruits. Burnt, grain, and wine offerings. Rest, no work.	Burnt and sin offerings. Rest, no work.	Burnt and sin offerings. Trumpet blasts. [d] Rest, no work.	Burnt, grain, and drink offerings. A complete fast. Rest, no work.	Burnt and sin offerings. Live in shelters. Rejoicing.
Scripture References	Exodus 12:1–14 Leviticus 23:5 Numbers 9:9–14; 28:16 Deuteronomy 16:1–8	Exodus 12:15–20; 13:3–10; 23:14–15 Leviticus 23:6–8 Numbers 28:17–25 Deuteronomy 16:1–8	Leviticus 23:9–14	Exodus 23:16; 34:22, 26 Leviticus 23:15–21 Numbers 28:26–31 Deuteronomy 16:9–12	Leviticus 23:23–25	Leviticus 23:26–32	Leviticus 23:33–43 Deuteronomy 16:13–17

a In addition to the Sabbath. See Leviticus 23:3.

b Because the dates are set according to the Jewish calendar, which is controlled by the phases of the moon, the dates vary from year to year in the Gregorian (today's) calendar.

c Pilgrimage festivals, meaning that all Jewish men were to come to Jerusalem to celebrate the festival. Some people consider Passover and Unleavened Bread to be one long event because they are next to each other.

d Unless it is on the Sabbath, in which case there are no trumpet blasts.

Timeline of Kings and Prophets

Years BC

Prophets are in italics. Their location on the table does not indicate the kingdom of their ministry. Since the time of the ministry of some of the prophets is uncertain, a question mark follows their name, and they appear two or three times.

Legend

GOOD	GOOD turned BAD
BAD	BAD turned GOOD

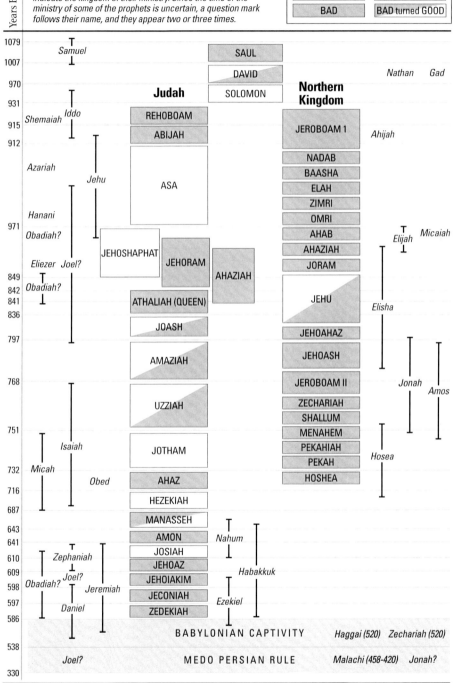

Years BC	Judah		Northern Kingdom	
1079		*Samuel*		
1007			SAUL	*Nathan* *Gad*
970			DAVID	
931		**Judah**	SOLOMON	**Northern Kingdom**
915	*Shemaiah* *Iddo*	REHOBOAM	JEROBOAM 1	*Ahijah*
912		ABIJAH	NADAB	
	Azariah		BAASHA	
	Jehu	ASA	ELAH	
			ZIMRI	
971	*Hanani*		OMRI	
	Obadiah?		AHAB	*Elijah* *Micaiah*
		JEHOSHAPHAT	AHAZIAH	
	Eliezer *Joel?*	JEHORAM AHAZIAH	JORAM	
849	*Obadiah?*			
842			JEHU	*Elisha*
841		ATHALIAH (QUEEN)		
836		JOASH	JEHOAHAZ	
797			JEHOASH	*Jonah*
768		AMAZIAH	JEROBOAM II	*Amos*
		UZZIAH	ZECHARIAH	
751			SHALLUM	
	Isaiah	JOTHAM	MENAHEM	
732	*Micah*		PEKAHIAH	*Hosea*
716		*Obed*	PEKAH	
687		AHAZ	HOSHEA	
		HEZEKIAH		
643		MANASSEH		
641		AMON	*Nahum*	
610	*Zephaniah*	JOSIAH		
609	*Joel?*	JEHOAZ	*Habakkuk*	
598	*Obadiah?* *Jeremiah*	JEHOIAKIM		
597	*Daniel*	JECONIAH	*Ezekiel*	
586		ZEDEKIAH		
		BABYLONIAN CAPTIVITY		*Haggai (520)* *Zechariah (520)*
538	*Joel?*	MEDO PERSIAN RULE		*Malachi (458-420)* *Jonah?*
330				

117

Translation Notes

Translation Type: The Readable Bible is a literal translation[a] in the sense that each original language word is expressed in English. However, sometimes a literal translation is unlikely to communicate the writer's thought to a modern audience. For instance, people unfamiliar with ancient culture probably do not understand that the term "kiss the Son" in Psalm 2:12 means to show him homage. So, where the literal translation might confuse or mislead today's reader, a thought-for-thought translation is presented and the literal translation is footnoted, or vice versa (unless the term is listed in "Nonliteral Words and Phrases Not Footnoted"). When an action verb is immediately followed by another action verb (e.g., "got up and went"), oftentimes only the second verb is expressed in the English text.

Added Words: Sometimes the author left out words that he knew his audience would have in their minds due to their familiarity with the context, culture, and language. Today English-speaking readers need those words added to the text. Thus, we supply them, as well as other explanatory words, in *italics*. Italicized additions are also made to clarify the text or avoid confusion for readers who (1) are not familiar with Scripture truths and the history of Israel and (2) might not recognize when figures of speech (e.g., hyperboles, metaphors) are being used.

Grammar: As is common in modern translations, the words are not always expressed in the grammatical form of the original text when that creates awkward English. Instead, the text is presented as we speak today. Occasionally, for clarity or ease of reading, we substitute a noun for a pronoun, or vice versa.

Hinneh: The Hebrew word *hinneh* calls attention to what follows. It indicates an emotional moment, brings focus upon a dialogue or a report, or expresses a person's reaction to a situation. While it is not directly translatable into English, "behold" is used in older translations, and "look" is used in more modern ones. The Readable Bible expresses it with a word or phrase such as "look," "notice," "pay attention," "believe me," "suddenly," and "was surprised to see." While it is common for modern translations to ignore the word, The Readable Bible almost always renders it.

Uncertain Translation: Many Hebrew words have several meanings. If an equally viable alternate term or phrase would give the text a significantly different sense or feel than the one given by the word we render, we provide the alternate in a notation.

Weights and Measures: Current equivalents are presented in rounded, easy-to-read amounts. The literal text is footnoted. The equivalents are uncertain because ancient measures varied by time and place, and archaeological information is incomplete. Coinage[b] can be expressed somewhat accurately in weight, but it is more difficult to translate its value into terms that relate accurately to today. The exact amount does not appear to be crucial to the meaning of any passage.

---

a The Old Testament translation is based primarily upon the Biblia Hebraica Stuttgartensia (BHS), 5th edition. Some passages are modified due to questionable BHS text and/or more recent manuscript discoveries. Such modifications draw from the Septuagint, Dead Sea Scrolls, Samaritan Pentateuch, Targums, and Syriac text. The Masoretic text is noted, as is the source of the modification.

b Until the first government-issued coinage was made in about 600 BC, coinage was simply pieces of metal used as a medium of exchange.

Format and Presentation Notes

The Readable Bible presents text that is as readable as any other twenty-first-century nonfiction work. Here are a few of the ways that is accomplished.

Callouts, Headings, Bold Type: These features help keep you oriented and aid information searches. Callout boxes and headings that are not part of sentences are not part of the inspired text. The words in boldface are not more important than any other words of the text.

Capitalization: Personal pronouns that refer to God are not capitalized unless necessary for clarity (as there is no such distinction in the original manuscripts). The term "spirit" is capitalized when it refers to God.

Contractions: Rather than adhere to modern literature standards such as MLA style or *Chicago Manual of Style*, the translation varies language style according to context. Contractions are used as they might normally be used by today's writers and speakers (i.e., inconsistently, not in every possible place but in many). This results in a more natural text that improves readability yet does not affect meaning.

Lists: Items in a series are sometimes presented in list format. These should be read down the first column and then down the next column.

Nonliteral Text: Words and phrases not translated literally and appearing more than three times in a book are not footnoted. Instead, the literal translation is provided in the "Nonliteral Words and Phrases Not Footnoted" table in the back of the book.

Quote Marks: Ancient writings used "said" to indicate a direct quotation. Today we use quotation marks for the same purpose. Thus, when the manuscript text reads, "The LORD spoke to Moses, saying, '[quote].'" The Readable Bible reads, "The LORD said to Moses, '[quote].'"

Slashes: The slash between words in a footnote represents "or" or "and/or."

Tables: Tables are used for object specifications, genealogies, census and other numerical data, and some lists. Table headings list the verses that are rendered solely in that table. This list does not include verses referenced in the table that are fully rendered in their normal location outside the table. Quantities in italics are calculated, not in the Hebrew text.

Verse numbers preceding table text refer to the following text until the next number. At times a verse number follows table text and applies to the text before and after it until the next entry with a verse number beside it.

Text Location: Some text has been moved to increase readability and clarity, to conform with modern paragraph construction practice, or to group like information in a single location. When text is moved to a different page, its chapter and verse(s) are noted in its new location, and its new location is noted in its original location. On occasion, adjacent verses are grouped together when sentences and phrases have been rearranged to conform to English composition norms.

Transliteration: When a transliterated proper noun first appears in the text, if its English translation adds clarity or meaning to the text, it is provided within parentheses like this: "Nod (*i.e.*, Wandering)."

Nonliteral Words and Phrases Not Footnoted

The Readable Bible oftentimes renders the word "said" as an equivalent word that expresses the inner dialogue and/or feeling and/or emotion with which the words were spoken (e.g., announced, asked, answered, called to/out, cautioned, claimed, complained, confirmed, continued, declared, directed, wondered).

We follow the normal English Bible translation practice of inserting words that are not in the Hebrew text at the start of a sentence to facilitate smooth reading (e.g., "so," "now," "then," "when," "rather"). Thus, "then" does not mean an event directly followed a preceding event, though it might have. The reader must use their own judgment based on context.

When a place-name occurs without part of its normal English title, we add the title (e.g., "Jordan" becomes "Jordan River"; "Negev" becomes "Negev Desert").

The literal translation of the dynamic expressions below are not footnoted when the dynamic translation occurs three or more times. Not all occurrences of the literal expressions below are translated dynamically.

Dynamic Translation (Nonliteral)	Literal Translation
[Country] e.g., Egypt	Land of [country], land of Egypt
In/on that day	It will come about on that day.
Israelites	House of Israel
[Name]ites	Clan/family of [Name]
Now	It shall come to pass.
Petition	Soften the face
Sight	Eyes
Temple	House of the LORD
When	It was when; it came about when

If you enjoyed this book, will you consider sharing the message with others?

Let us know your thoughts. You can let the author know by visiting or sharing a photo of the cover on our social media pages or leaving a review at a retailer's site. All of it helps us get the message out!

Email: info@ironstreammedia.com

 @ironstreammedia

Brookstone Publishing Group, Iron Stream, Iron Stream Fiction, Iron Stream Harambee, Iron Stream Kids, and Life Bible Study are imprints of Iron Stream Media, which derives its name from Proverbs 27:17, "As iron sharpens iron, so one person sharpens another." This sharpening describes the process of discipleship, one to another. With this in mind, Iron Stream Media provides a variety of solutions for churches, ministry leaders, and nonprofits ranging from in-depth Bible study curriculum and Christian book publishing to custom publishing and consultative services.

For more information on ISM and its imprints, please visit
IronStreamMedia.com